# Caring Conversations

*Uncomfortable But Essential Questions*
*To Help You Navigate*
*Life's Biggest Disruptions*

Daniel & Nancy Nicewonger
*with friends*

# CONTENTS

Copyright                                          vii
Introduction                                       xiii
Caring for the Dying                               xix

## PART ONE
## RELATIONSHIPS

1. Perspectives                                     3
2. Support Circles                                  9
3. CONVERSATIONS WITH YOUNG FAMILIES               15
   with Chris Lawrence

4. WHAT CHILDREN SEE                               23
   with Rayann Nicewonger

5. Life Partners                                   31
   How Do I Feel?                                  37

## PART TWO
## FINANCIAL / LEGAL

6. REGAINING CONTROL                               41
   with Michael R. Perna

7. FINANCES                                        49
   with Paul Maynor

8. Insurance                                       57

9. PREPARING TO AVOID CHAOS AMIDST
   DISRUPTIONS                                     63
   with John L. Blair

   Can Fear Be My Friend?                          69

## PART THREE
## DAY-TO-DAY REALITIES

10. Navigating the Healthcare System     75
11. Technology / Social Media     83
12. Vehicles     91
13. Where Can It Be?     95
     Silent Tears     101

## PART FOUR
## HOME SWEET HOME

14. HOME HISTORY     105
     with Christina Reid

15. General Maintenance     113
16. Can I Live Here Alone?     119
     What is Strength?     123

## PART FIVE
## END-OF-LIFE ISSUES

17. Making The Most Of Your Time     127
18. Where Does My Stuff Go?     133
19. When Time Is Short     141
20. HOSPICE     147
     with Joan Holliday

     Caring Through Isolation     155

## PART SIX
## WHEN YOU THINK ABOUT ME

21. GRIEF IS HARD – BUT NECESSARY     159
     with Pastor Annalie Korengel

22. LEARNING TO BE A HEALTHY GRIEVER     169
     with Chaplain Tony Tilford

23. HELPING LOVED ONES GRIEVE     175
     with Matt Grieco

     Loving Through Long-Term Illness     181

## PART SEVEN
## SPIRITUAL JOURNEY

24. A Journey Like No Other                          187

    In Closing                                       199
    Contributors                                     203
    Permissions                                      205
    Notes                                            207

ISBN: 979-8390727584

Cover photo iStock.com/fizkes

*I (Dan) dedicate this book to my caregiver, Nancy. The years since we first heard "stage IV colon cancer" have not been easy. However, your presence has made the hard times manageable. Thank you for walking alongside me and carrying me when I need it. The past few years have been full of activity; none of it would have been possible without your support. Thank you.*

*The strength and grace with which you have carried the burdens of this journey humble me. It reminds me of what attracted me to you all those years ago. I have learned I love you more than I imagined possible.*

*Nancy and Dan dedicate this book to all the caregivers. Thank you for giving of yourselves to provide support and encouragement in some of life's darkest times. May you always find time for yourself, moments to renew your strength.*

*Nancy and Dan dedicate this book to Dr. Saroha and all the nurses and staff at Abramson Cancer Center. You model compassionate caregiving. We arrived as patients and found friends. Thank you.*

# CARING CONVERSATIONS

# INTRODUCTION

In May 2016, our world was turned upside down. One Thursday evening, I felt a twinge in my shoulder. It was the first sign of anything being wrong. Three days later, an oncologist told us I had stage IV colon cancer. Standing at the foot of my hospital bed, he told me the "outlook was not good; it was time to go home and get my affairs in order."

As he left my room Nancy and I were distraught and overwhelmed. Every conversation became much more intentional. We wanted to squeeze the most out of every moment we had together. At the same time, we realized some pressing issues needed to be talked about. We tried to balance taking care of business and simply enjoying time together.

Over time, Nancy and I started noting all our awkward conversations. Learning to discuss decisions regarding "prolonging life" and "quality of life" the same way we used to plan a vacation has not been easy. It is often painful, and we have learned the signs when the other needs a break from such weighty conversations.

Over time we started talking about how having a resource to guide our conversations would have been helpful. A roadmap of sorts to help us focus on what was important to discuss and share while fighting a terminal illness.

Nancy and I believe God can transform life's most difficult experiences for good. We have seen that truth lived out in our lives repeatedly. This book is the latest example of God transforming a brutal reality into something positive.

Many things can disrupt our lives. For us, it was a diagnosis of stage IV colon cancer and the recommendation to get one's affairs in order. However, the disruption in your life will most likely be something different.

As we got to work living one day at a time, sometimes one conversation at a time, we discovered a pathway forward. A pathway filled with hope and promise. We pray that you will find comfort in knowing others have navigated seasons of disruption. May your conversations be filled with grace and joy even in the darkest times.

## A Word from Barbara

Early in Dan's cancer journey, a caregiver support group was started at our church. This group gave me (Nancy) an outlet to share the challenges and joys of caring for my husband during his illness. One of the first things I noticed was that each caregiver had a unique approach that suited themselves and their loved ones.

A frequent topic I would share with the caregiver group was how Dan and I would have uncomfortable conversations about when/if he would die. I often shared out of a place of distress.

I accompanied Dan to the funeral home to plan his service. I left the funeral home with a migraine, a common occurrence during these conversations. Dan and I discussed insurance plans and hospice care scenarios. While Dan entered these conversations with my best interest in mind, I often resisted. Even to this day, writing this book, I often walk away in the middle of the conversation because I can only think of what is lurking in the future for a short time.

During caregiver group, I would share my sadness over why Dan and I needed to have these discussions. Listening as the group responded to my sharing, I realized that for some, the loved one does not want to discuss the realities of the illness. For others, a discussion of death seems out of the question and inappropriate. Dan and I talked about most topics related to his illness, the possibility of death, and my life without him.

One friend in our caregiver group, Barbara, often attended alongside her husband, Bill. Bill and Barbara had an outlook of hope. This was not Bill's first serious illness, and they went through the obstacles of treatments as partners, always looking to the future. Barbara responded to one of my sharings, saying, "We don't talk about things like that because Bill is not going to die from this." Then, a few years later, Barbara suddenly lost Bill and shared her experiences. She told me then, "There are things I need to know."

After sharing with Barbara the idea of this book and having intentional caring   conversations with our loved one, Barbara shared the following:

> *I wish I had had this book when my husband was sick. He contracted cancer in the Fall of 2014 and eventually had a bone marrow transplant. That worked, and the leukemia was gone. Perhaps we just thought everything would go well, so we didn't have many of the conversations this book advises. We should have had them!*
>
> *Even if all went well, it's important for all of us to understand our homes, our insurance policies, and every other piece of information that would be helpful in an emergency or a change in health. A stroke took my husband from our family, and it took me a long time just to discover what I needed to know. Please read this book, take notes on what you learn, and enjoy the times you have together.* [1]

Serious illness is difficult. It can be time-consuming and overwhelming. However, information and knowledge can be a help. I hope the following chapters give you food for thought about how to travel this journey with your loved one.

## How to use this book

We have worked to set this book up as an easy-to-use resource. Our sense is that if you are looking at this amid your disruption, the last thing you have time to do is read a book telling you what to do or how to feel.

Disruptions require responses, immediate responses, and we have little energy left for personal growth exercises. So rather than provide answers, we thought the most helpful thing we could do was ask questions. Ask the kind of questions that got us talking about the crucial issues that must be discussed amid the disruption of a significant life event.

You certainly could read the book from beginning to end. We believe you would find value in that exercise. We also believe you could use it as a guidebook of sorts. When a particular issue arises, find the relevant chapter and use the questions to help guide your conversations. Some questions will require a little research or reflection. However, many are designed to help you think about how you and those near you navigate the disruption in your life.

However you choose to use the book, we believe you will find value in having deeper conversations in the midst of chaos.

## The voices that speak

One afternoon Nancy and I went out for lunch to discuss this project. In a few short minutes, we had the outline for what we wanted to share. Remembering our journey, friends and supporters came to mind. Paul is our financial advisor, and our meeting with him post-diagnosis was extremely helpful. Matt is a good friend who happens to be a funeral director; sitting and discussing funeral arrangements helped me (Dan) get on with living. Joan has decades of experience as a community nurse, and Chris is a top-notch real estate agent. Our lawyer, Michael, ensured all our legal affairs were handled. Annalie and Tony have spent decades helping those who are grieving. Rayann, our daughter, was sixteen when I was diagnosed.

What if each one added their expertise to relevant chapters? As the project progressed, a few other voices were added. Each adds value and helps us think more clearly about navigating life's disruptions well. We were blessed to have everyone respond with excitement and an offer to help. This resource is richer for their wisdom. You can find a complete list of their names and contact information in the book's final chapter.

Most chapters begin with a few words from Nancy or myself. We introduce the topic and share a little about how we navigated this part of our journey. A "line" separates the voices of our friends so you know when they begin to share. In a few chapters, Nancy and I will add some final thoughts. Again our words are separated by a "line", so you know the voices have changed.

# CARING FOR THE DYING
## – HENRI NOUWEN

Caring for others is, first of all, helping them to overcome that enormous temptation of self-rejection. Whether we are rich or poor, famous or unknown, fully abled or disabled, we all share the fear of being left alone and abandoned, a fear that remains hidden under the surface of our self-composure. It is rooted much more deeply than in the possibility of not being liked or loved by people. Its deepest root lies in the possibility of not being loved at all, of not belonging to anything that lasts, or being swallowed up by a dark nothingness—yes, of being abandoned by God.

Caring, therefore, is being present to people as they fight this ultimate battle, a battle that becomes evermore real and intense as death approaches. Dying and death always call forth, with renewed power, the fear that we are unloved and will, finally, be reduced to useless ashes. To care is to stand by a dying person and to be a living reminder that the person is indeed the beloved child of God. . . .

We shouldn't try to care by ourselves. Care is not an endurance test. We should, whenever possible, care together with others. It is the community of care that reminds the dying person of his or her belovedness. [1]

# PART ONE
# RELATIONSHIPS

Life's disruptions come in many forms. But, whatever the disruption, it introduces anxiety and stress into our lives. Life has taken a turn, the future is unsure, and we begin to question much that we once thought secure.

Our personal relationships are among the first places we feel the impact of such a disruption. Each member of our family unit is experiencing the disruption in slightly different ways. While they may be aware of our struggle, friends and co-workers are often consumed with their own lives.

Navigating our relationships well during a season of disruption takes intention and focus. If you are like Nancy and me, this will be a season where you grow and learn much about yourself. You will find strength you never knew existed deep within yourself. You will be surprised by who comes alongside you to provide support and encouragement. Equally surprising will be those who cannot face the reality of your disruption and seem to fade into the mist. The key is to remember that everyone is experiencing and responding to the disruption in their way. Rarely is someone's comment, reaction, or lack of involvement a personal slight. It has more to do with how they are processing (or not processing) the trauma of the disruption.

Spending time thinking about your relationships and how to navigate them in a healthy way is time well spent. Focus less on the response and reaction of others and more on how you can walk this season well.

# PERSPECTIVES

My caregiver (Nancy) and I have traveled a similar journey as I have battled cancer. I could not have asked for a better partner for the journey these past few years. Nancy has made everything I have accomplished possible. She has helped me through difficult times and strengthened me when I was tired of the fight. Nancy has been a fantastic partner, yet we see things through different lenses. I must remind myself that we have different perspectives.

Nancy and I were both in the room when we first met Dr. Saroha. Nancy sat in a chair; I lay in my bed as we first heard, "You have cancer." We were less than four feet apart, yet we were separated by miles. I listened to words that caused me to think about my mortality. Nancy heard the exact same words and wondered what life would be like without me. Perspectives.

We have walked every inch of this journey together. Every momentous decision has been made together. Yet we still see things very differently.

Part of "finishing well" or "quality of life" means making the most of my remaining time. Living in such a way means that when

I have energy, I am often busy. Nancy sees all the activity and wonders if I ought to slow down. She can't help but think that somehow all this activity damages my body and takes time off my life. We have talked about it. We asked Dr. Saroha, and he assured us it was not causing me any harm. Still, I can see the question in her eyes as she looks at me. We are two people living a shared experience and having very different perspectives.

One of my goals over the past few years has been to clear out some of the stuff I no longer need or use. A while back, I sold a very nice fly-tying station. A few years ago, I got interested in fly fishing. I tend to go "all in" on things and decided I needed to learn how to make my flies. So, out in my shop, I custom-made a fly-tying stand. It was the Cadillac of fly-tying stations. It has been years since I last went fly-fishing, even longer since I tied my last fly. Something about being unsteady on solid ground made me question the wisdom of standing in a rushing river. It was time for the stand to find a new home.

When the buyer came to pick it up, I was excited. But, looking at Nancy, I could tell she had a different perspective. "Each time you sell something like this, it feels like you are letting a piece of you go. It makes me sad."

I was fine moving away from these things. I saw them as things. In truth, I viewed what I was doing as helpful. If I did not do this now, there might come a day when Nancy is left to take care of a basement full of items she knows little about. Instead of being thankful, Nancy watched them go and was grieving the changes cancer had brought upon me—different perspectives.

It is hard for a caregiver to watch the transformation cancer (or any illness) can bring upon one they love. While traveling on the same journey, their perspective will be different.

If you know someone serving as a caregiver, take a moment and ask them how they are doing. Ask for their perspective on the journey. Your question will help them as much as their answer will bless you.

## QUESTIONS TO HELP TALK ABOUT DIFFERENT PERSPECTIVES:

- What has been the biggest blessing while on this journey?
- What has been the biggest challenge?
- How has your perspective changed while journeying through your disruption?
- When do you and your caregiver/care receiver talk about how you are each experiencing this journey?
- I wish my partner (caregiver/care receiver) knew _____ about my experience of this journey.
- Even though I do not understand, I need to be more sensitive toward my caregiver/care receiver's feelings in this area: _____.
- What is one thing that would make your piece of the journey easier? How can you share that with others near you?
- Who do you talk with, other than your caregiver/care receiver, about the journey?
- Thinking about those closest to you, family, friends, and co-workers, what is their perspective of the journey through your disruption?
- Thinking about those closest to you, family, friends, and co-workers, how do you view the disruptions in their lives?

# SUPPORT CIRCLES

As I (Nancy) drove away from the hospital, I felt like my world was collapsing. My 47-year-old husband was diagnosed with stage 4 cancer. The task of telling everyone was left to me. My children. His parents. My family. The leadership of the church. Everyone we knew. I was overwhelmed.

On the way home, I called my brother. We rarely talked, but he knew Dan was in the hospital and answered immediately. I gave Todd, my older brother, the job of calling my parents, sister, and a few others. It was more than I could handle. I knew if I heard the voices of my mom and dad, I would fall apart. So, I dumped it on my brother. Sometimes, that is how we can use support.

In actuality, this disruption has brought Dan and me closer to Todd, or Parney, as he is known to the rest of the world. Todd gathered the information and clarified what details were public and what was private, even from family. I did not want the stage level talked about, so I gave more general cancer information. Todd told family members when and how to contact me the following day. My parents graciously accepted this plan and did not mind that I used support to get through this challenging task of disclosing the diagnosis.

Over the years, I have had a few close friends with whom I could discuss what I wanted when/if "something happens to Dan." One friend has been tasked with making sure I am not alone the first hours after Dan passes away. Within my family, when someone dies, family and friends show up at the house over the next few days and spend time there. Unfortunately, I do not have extended family in the area, and my parents can no longer travel to my home for any circumstance. So I have asked a friend to arrange for friends to surround me when needed.

A few years later, a friend of mine lost her husband unexpectedly. I offered to go over to sit with her. She declined, wanting to be alone. I honored that request because it was what she felt was best. Support means different things to different people. Defining what is best for me can make a difference as I go through challenges and grief.

THE FOLLOWING QUESTIONS ARE DESIGNED TO HELP YOU THINK ABOUT WHAT KIND OF SUPPORT YOU MIGHT FIND MOST HELPFUL AND WHERE YOU MIGHT FIND IT:

IN THE BEGINNING:

- What support do you need at the beginning of the disruption?
- How can you share information in a way that is safe for you?
- Do you need physical support such as meals, transportation, or other help?

- Is it hard for you to receive help? Will declining help early on make people less likely to offer help in the future?
- Are there specific areas of expertise you need help navigating (legal, financial, medical advocacy, housing, food insecurity, etc.)? Who might direct you to the right place to find help?

## DURING A PROLONGED ILLNESS:

- Would you benefit from a support group consisting of others in a similar situation?
- Would you benefit from counseling?
- Will you need help physically caring for your loved one?
- Do you need physical support such as meals or transportation?
- Who can help you make decisions?
- Who can help you share information with family and friends?
- What support will you need during the end of the illness?
- Who can you call in the middle of the night when you don't want to be alone?
- Who can come to the funeral and minimize conflicts?

## WHEN YOUR LOVED ONE PASSES AWAY

- Chances are you will find many people willing to support you during the days and weeks following a death. But can you ask someone to walk alongside you for a more extended season?

- Often, caregivers are caught up with the urgent demands of caring for the one they love. Taking time to build support circles will ensure you do not walk alone during this challenging season. Who are the people you would want walking closely with you? Have you shared that with them?
- Be open to finding support from unexpected places and people. Take a moment and think about those who have supported you. Who has surprised you with their level of caring? Might you find a way to deepen that relationship?

# CONVERSATIONS WITH YOUNG FAMILIES

## WITH CHRIS LAWRENCE

I (Dan) met Chris while traveling on my cancer journey. He is the founder and executive director of Hope Has Arrived. Hope Has Arrived is focused on helping cancer patients and their loved ones find hope amid one of life's biggest disruptions.

Chris had come across our book, *The Journey Continues* and wanted to talk about my story. Over the past few years, we have worked together on several projects.

Chris's story is an amazing one. His disruption came in the form of a cancer diagnosis when he was newly married and with a young child. I thought it important to hear the perspective of a young person faced with a significant disruption.

When I was first diagnosed with cancer, one of my (Chris Lawrence's) greatest fears was what would happen to my family if I died.

Like many people, hearing I had cancer greatly shocked me and upended my life. Yet, the hardest part for me was being diagnosed at a relatively young age with a young family: a wife and a six-month-old daughter.


## MY STORY

I began having unexplained back pain in the fall of 2015, which I thought was just a sports injury. I was only thirty-seven years old, and as a husband and new father, I worked for an outdoor program in Colorado. I loved my life, but it seemed everything would soon be taken from me.

My wife, Elizabeth, and I had both waited until our thirties to get married. My grandparents had recently celebrated seventy years of marriage together. If I'm honest, I hoped that Elizabeth and I might be able to be married that long, too (I know, the math doesn't add up).

Yet, just three years into our marriage, I was diagnosed with stage IV bile duct cancer, which is incurable and has a life expectancy of 1-1.5 years. It seemed like our hopes and dreams for our future were shattered.

Dealing with cancer and its potential to cut a life short is difficult for people of any age. But at least from my perspective, one of the most painful aspects was being ripped away from a family we were just starting.

I think other young families wrestle with this, too. How do you comprehend the potential impact of a life cut short by cancer? So much of your life with your family is supposed to be in front of you?

## AWKWARD CONVERSATIONS

Talking through such topics can prove awkward and perhaps even hope killing. I remember when Elizabeth and I tried to talk about it a few times. The conversations felt weird and dark. It's because we were discussing my potential death. The very idea was difficult to contemplate.

However, I think it is important to think about the future and have a plan. Even if you don't have cancer, it is wise to consider what will happen to your family if either parent dies. It's why life insurance was created and why assigning godparents is wise.

I am certainly no expert on having these conversations, and I wish I had done them better. However, if I could share some helpful thoughts about what to keep in mind when you have these conversations, here is what I would say:

1. **Be willing to have difficult conversations**. I believe not talking about the potential of what could happen might have increased the fear for my wife and me. As distasteful as it may feel to talk about the future, it may prove worse or increase the fear of it if you don't. So have the conversations.

2. **Plan for the future.** Everyone's life is uncertain, whether you have cancer or not. Yet, when you get a diagnosis, especially a life-limiting one, it is wise to consider the what-ifs of the future and plan accordingly. Things like life insurance, godparents, hospice, funeral, getting finances in order, etc., are important. But don't just plan for your potential death. Instead, plan for what you want to do with the rest of your life. For example, plan how you want to spend your time as a family and how to create lasting memories together.

3. **Live every day as a gift.** This is not just a cheap sentiment. The truth is that every day we have life, and breath is a gift from God. Choose to see every day as a gift and enjoy them. Living with gratitude will help you live in the moment, use your time well, and be present with your loved ones.

4. **Let go of control.** Know that no medical textbook or doctor determines the number of your days; only God does. No one can predict precisely how long you will live, and many people defy what statistics say. So, please stop trying to control your life. Instead, embrace each day and live it the best you can. Life can still be beautiful and good, even if it is fragile and uncertain.

5. **Ask for prayer or pray.** When facing desperate times and difficult realities, it is good and right to ask for wisdom and guidance from God. As the saying goes, there are no atheists in foxholes. When facing difficult times is a great time to ask others to pray for you and your family or even to reach out to God yourself. If you do so, know that many others have the same desire. _Asking God for Help_ is currently one of the most popular articles on my website, www.hopehasarrived.com.

6. **Don't live in the worst-case scenario.** In other words, just because you or your loved one was given a life-limiting diagnosis, it is not a certainty about the future. New medical breakthroughs in the cancer world are flipping the script on what used to be death sentences. Some people defy a diagnosis, even without the latest treatment. Know that there are plenty of reasons to keep hope alive.

7. **Choose to live in hope.** God gives us a hope that can never be defeated. While we all will lose the hope of living in this life at some point, it does not mean we have to lose hope. Instead, we come to appreciate a hope that was always the strongest of all: eternal hope. In other words, the hope that God loves us, that we can be with him now and spend eternity with him in heaven after our time on earth.

## THE REST OF MY STORY

So, the rest of my story proved a bit unexpected. A few months after my diagnosis, God provided a cancer research doctor who tried a new approach to treat my cancer, and it worked. I have now been in remission for six years and counting. Thankfully this approach has become widely available in cancer care.

Yet, like everyone, I don't know my future, but I continue to make the most of each day and live my life as a gift.

I will never forget the perspective of facing death. I realized the power of hope and how it is like the air we breathe. And I know that when the day comes when I face death again, I will do so with a hope that will go beyond just life on this earth.

I believe this hope helped my wife and I get better at having the necessary conversations about complex subjects, like the end of life.

I encourage others, if you have not broached these subjects, maybe today is a good day to start. Beyond that, choose to live in hope and live each day as a gift. Doing this will help us make the best of the time we have been given.

Chris Lawrence is the founder of *Hope Has Arrived*, a nonprofit which helps all people find hope, strength, and peace against cancer. For more help on your cancer journey, check out hopehasarrived.com.

## QUESTIONS FOR YOUNG FAMILIES:

- Do you have life insurance? This simple step can help provide security for your family in the case of a disruption.
- Have you arranged for guardians who will care for your children in case both you and your spouse pass before they are adults?
- If you have arranged for guardians, have you communicated your wishes with close family? Some people opt not to share that information, hoping it is never needed. In contrast, others proactively seek to eliminate potential conflicts.
- Does your will clearly identify who you intend the guardians to be? In some states, if you do not provide clear instructions, the state can/may become involved in making decisions regarding your children. This is especially true if both parents should pass away.

When thinking about clearly defining your wishes regarding minor children, our (Dan & Nancy) lawyer, Michael R. Perna, added: "By leaving such instructions, even in states where guardianship courts are not bound to follow them (because the 'best interest of the child' standard trumps testamentary instructions), this is the best way to let the court know your wishes—which it will most definitely take into consideration."

# WHAT CHILDREN SEE
## WITH RAYANN NICEWONGER

Rayann has been living with us through most of this journey. She has had a "front-row seat" to the struggles and joys. Joseph had already launched into the world and caught only glimpses from visits and phone calls. As we put the book together, I (Dan) asked Rayann if she might want to write a chapter dealing with how long-term illness impacts children who find themselves a part of the journey. Her words humble me. It is crucial to make sure nobody "gets lost" in the midst of one of life's disruptions. Nancy and I could have helped her navigate this season better if someone had communicated what she shares with you now.

~

I was 16 when I came home from school, and my Mom told me that my Dad had cancer. I could describe that day for you in great detail. What I was wearing, what I did after school, the text from Mom asking me to meet her at home, what I said after the words "they found out he has cancer" left her mouth, and how everything

I thought I could count on was ripped from my hands in five minutes. Over the past seven years, I have learned a lot about how a diagnosis like cancer can affect the children involved.

## BALANCE OF SHARING INFORMATION:

I left home for a semester abroad in January 2020. When I left, everything was good. Dad had surgery back in November for a new treatment, but he hadn't started it yet. He was going to start while I was gone. I talked to my parents regularly while I was away. I knew he was having some issues, but the full extent of the problem was not shared with me. When I came home in March 2020, I expected to see him at the airport. When I got there, I found out that he had been in the hospital for a couple of days and that they didn't know what was wrong. Things were serious. Serious enough that the thought that I wouldn't get the chance to tell him about my trip was running through my mind.

I felt blindsided and was frustrated that I wasn't told the whole story while I was gone. I understand why my parents didn't tell me. They wanted me to enjoy my trip and not worry, but coming home was made harder because I was hit with everything all at once. I felt blindsided by what I was walking into. There's a balance between sharing too much and sharing too little. Having an honest conversation about where that line is would be beneficial. You don't want to weigh your children down if they are younger, but you don't want to leave them in the dark. It's probably a conversation you'll want to have more than once. As time goes on, they might want to know more or less.

## NOT WHAT THEY PICTURED:

My Dad is my guy. One of the hardest things about him being sick was realizing that he might not be there for everything that I wanted him to be at. Everyone has an idea about who they want with them at certain events. They might have pictured someone else, their other parent; being there for certain things and adjusting to the new reality is complicated. I went to an accepted students day at my future college about a year after my Dad was diagnosed. I was nervous, and my Dad is the one I like to have with me when I'm uneasy about situations. I remember sitting in the auditorium thinking, " I want Dad here." I had nothing against my Mom being there, but I had always thought he would be with me at things like that. It was hard sitting there and knowing Dad wasn't there because he was sick. It was an adjustment and another thing that I felt cancer had taken from me. I was upset and frustrated at the time, and I'm sure my Mom had no idea why. There will be moments to understand that your children are not upset that you are there but simply that someone else is missing.

## HOW ARE YOU DOING?

One frustrating part of my Dad's cancer has been that sometimes I feel invisible. When people would talk to me, the conversation went like this, "How is your Dad doing? How is your Mom doing? Tell them I'm thinking about them!" I would leave these conversations feeling irritated. Why didn't they ask how I was? No, I'm not the one with cancer or the one who is the primary caregiver in this situation, but I was the sixteen-year-old whose world was flipped upside down. I was struggling, and there were times when I felt like that didn't matter or that I wasn't important. I would advise asking your children how they are dealing with everything. Maybe even ask someone else to check in on them. They might be more willing to share with someone who isn't directly involved.

## COUNSELING:

Meeting with a counselor is one of the most beneficial things I have done. I've always had a hard time talking about my Dad's cancer to people. I felt it was depressing and didn't want to be a downer. Then, about two years into his cancer journey, my Dad suggested that I start meeting with someone. His point was that when he died, I would already have a relationship with someone who understood what had gone on during his cancer. I started meeting with a counselor soon after. It was amazing to me. Finally, there was someone I felt I could say anything to without judgment. Someone whom I could work through things with. My counselor also helped me process what had already happened and helped me really understand how it had affected me. I felt like I could say things to her that I couldn't say to my parents or my friends, and that was important.

## PLANS CHANGE:

When I thought about college before Dad got sick, my main requirement was that I would be at least 5 hours away from home. I made this plan pretty clear to my parents. My Dad got sick at the end of my junior year in high school, right when I was starting to really think about college. All along, my Dad has always said that he doesn't want his cancer to affect my life choices and get in the way of my plans. It took me about two months to decide I wanted to live at home for college. I remember when I told my Dad, one of his first questions was, "Are you doing this because of me?" The answer wasn't black and white. Yes, a part of me changed my plans because he was sick. The doctors said he had about two years to live when he was first diagnosed. I decided that I wasn't going to spend my last two years with him away at college with a few phone calls a week and some weekend trips home. I knew I would be upset with myself later in life if that was how I spent my last years with him. There were a few other reasons to change my plans, but that was the driving reason. My Mom told me later that he was really concerned that I was making that choice just because of him. Her response to him was along the lines of "It's her choice to decide how she wants to spend these next few years." I think she knew that cancer was affecting this decision but that, at the end of the day, it was my choice to make. Your kids might change their plans too. Letting them make that choice is important.

## SOME QUESTIONS RAYANN PUT TOGETHER FOR YOU TO CONSIDER AS YOU HELP CHILDREN NAVIGATE ONE OF LIFE'S DISRUPTIONS:

- Do my children really need to know this piece of information about the disruption? Will it just put unnecessary stress on them?
- If I don't share this detail now, will it come back later and be harder to share? Will it make my children feel like I'm hiding things from them?
- Am I telling family and friends this? Is there any chance my children might hear it from someone else?
- If I don't share all the details, will my children understand enough of what is happening?
- Am I acknowledging that this disruption is hard on them too?
- Are people asking how my children are doing?
- Is there someone I could ask to check in on my children? Someone to ask them how they are doing on a regular basis.
- Do I think counseling would be beneficial for my children? Do they think counseling would be beneficial?

- Do my children talk openly and freely to me or anyone else?
- Do I think my children are making choices because it's what they think is best? They might feel like they have no control right now. Would letting them make this choice give them some sense of control back?
- Have you told your children you don't want them changing plans just because of you? Should you share your opinion on their choice but let them make their decision?

# LIFE PARTNERS

Nancy and I stood before family and friends on June 2, 1990, to boldly declare our love for each other. We had graduated college just a few short weeks prior. As we spoke the words "till death do us part," we felt invincible. We were not thinking about the struggles of life. There was a party to attend, and then we were off on our honeymoon.

Years later, our love has only deepened. It has not all been easy. Nancy and I can talk about "the vacation that saved our marriage." Life was complicated. We had drifted apart. We were functioning less as partners and more as unrelated characters in the same story. A few weeks away with our young family helped us focus on each other and the love that brought us together. We both knew things were changing for the better during that vacation. It was not till years later that we spoke of "the vacation that saved our marriage."

My diagnosis has led to significant changes within our relationship. Roles and responsibilities have shifted. Some of what used to be my (Dan's) job to take care of simply falls outside my physical ability. In addition, facing my mortality caused me to shift priorities. I found that some things were no longer important, while others took on a real sense of urgency. Nancy was trying to survive the chaos of the moment while I was formulating a plan as to how I would finish my life well.

Learning to care for, nurture, and love each other while walking this road has not always been easy. Nancy wants to rush to my side and help when I am fighting against feeling helpless. How does one help when I am unsure of what I want or need? There was a time when the drugs I was on made it difficult for me to button a shirt. Listen to how I wrote about that season in December 2016,

> *My neuropathy is not getting better. I have a hard time with buttons. I used to take buttoning my shirt for granted. A simple task at the start of each day. Today it is a monumental process worthy of celebration once complete. Nancy wants to help. "I do NOT need help buttoning my shirt!" I am a grown man; I can handle this, have been ever since I was a toddler. Nancy stands back and watches me struggle. "Aren't you going to help?" Nancy gets sneaky and buttons half the buttons on my shirt before she lays it out for me. As I pull the shirt over my head, I am reminded of how much she cares. I am reminded of how much she cares AND the reality that I cannot dress myself efficiently and effectively. The frustration is real, and I must be careful about sharing it with those around me.* [1]

In a very real way, we were forced to learn a new way of relating. The truth is my illness impacted every area of our relationship.

When I was first diagnosed, I was extremely weak. The chemotherapy left me even weaker. It was all I could do to make it through each day. Physical expressions of love, past holding hands or a short hug, were beyond my ability. When my body hit the bed each night, I just shut down. This was not the normal pattern for our relationship. Nancy never complained, but I could tell she was struggling. Physical distance was yet another change cancer was bringing to our lives.

A few months into treatment and I could tell the chemotherapy was changing something. My energy levels increased, and I no longer passed out when my head hit the pillow. One evening Nancy and I returned to a familiar pattern of expressing our love for each other. Laying beside each other, she whispered, "I thought I had lost that part of you forever." While not lost forever, our physical expressions of love have certainly evolved. Cancer and seven years of chemotherapy have left me a little different than the man Nancy married right out of college.

Why do we feel this is important to include in this book? Well, if you are lucky enough to have a partner to travel a journey such as this with, you will want to pay attention to the relationship. Disruptions such as serious illness, loss of a loved one, or any trauma will test even the strongest of relationships.

In times of chaos, we tend to look for those closest to us to remain strong and consistent. We draw the courage to face uncertainty from what we perceive as their strength. If they appear to be changing, we can feel betrayed at the very moment we need them most. It is important to understand that every area of a relationship will experience changes while you deal with one of life's disruptions.

Nancy and I can share about our relationship. We know nothing of the relationships you have invested in. We can, however, ask a few questions that may help you strengthen your relationships as you walk a season of disruption.

## QUESTIONS TO HELP STRENGTHEN YOUR RELATIONSHIP DURING A SEASON OF DISRUPTION:

- How do you express love/care for those closest to you? How has that changed since the diagnosis or disruption?
- How do those closest to you express love/care for you? How has that changed since the diagnosis or disruption?
- As you think about your closest relationships, how have they been strengthened during this season? What could you say or do to help strengthen them further?
- What do you wish your partner would do or say to help make this journey more manageable? Would they do/say it if you shared that it would be helpful?
- Have you asked your partner how you might best support them during this season? Remember that your partner's world is changing just as fast as yours. What might have been helpful six months ago may no longer be helpful.

# How Do I Feel?

People have asked how I feel. It has been nineteen days since my husband was diagnosed with cancer. Nineteen days since the oncologist sat with us in the hospital and explained the realities of Dan's cancer.

How do I feel? My heart has been breaking.

Next week we will have our 26th anniversary. I told Dan years ago I wanted to make it to our 65th. That is probably no longer a reality. My heart is breaking.

When the doctor left the hospital room, Dan's mind immediately went to what his cancer would mean to me and our children. A tear would stream down his face each time. My heart would break with each tear.

Pain has taken a new place in Dan's life. He has struggled with his breathing. He cannot do what he enjoys or what simply needs to be done. I have been driving us around, which does not normally happen. I have been going to doctor appointments to ask questions for him, which he does not normally need. For him, my heart breaks.

Do I have faith during this struggle? I do. But that does not keep me from feeling sad. People have told me that God will heal, and I need to stop worrying about it. I'm not exactly worrying about it. I am watching my husband suffer, and my heart is breaking.

I believe within my heartache, I am still trusting God. I do have a peace that God is in control. Jesus, while on earth, showed sadness at times. God knows the plans he has for me, but my heart is still broken.

God will mend my heart. So many people are praying for Dan. God may bring a miracle into his life and wipe away the cancer. Chemotherapy may do what the doctor said was not possible and bring a complete cure. God can restore Dan's health and mend my broken heart.

People don't want to hear that I must come to grips with the reality of cancer. But, for the sake of myself and my children and even for Dan, I need to be aware of what could happen. And if it does, God will protect and provide for us, and somehow we will survive. God will somehow mend my broken heart, but still, it will be very, very broken.

My trust in God will see me through this chapter in my life. Nineteen days after the diagnosis, my focus is more on daily life and less on possibilities. It is more on our blessings and less on what may be. As a result, I can enjoy each day and store more memories in my heart. Healing is already taking place.

How am I doing? As Dan has been saying: God is good all the time. All the time, God is good. [1]

# PART TWO
# FINANCIAL / LEGAL

When disruptions come our way, financial and legal concerns tend to fall into two categories. First, some concerns become real immediately and demand swift action. Things such as the loss of income or legal issues we cannot avoid fall into this first category.

In the second category are those things we know are essential, but somehow we feel it is okay to wait until another day to address them. A disruption's emotional and physical realities can make it easy for us to say, "when things calm down, I will get to the financial and legal issues." Again, it helps to know how you tend to navigate life. If you are a "put it off till the last minute" type of person, chances are this is how you will look at financial and legal issues in the midst of a disruption.

This might be an opportunity to invite someone to come alongside you and provide support and assistance. Someone who can focus on the critical financial and legal issues confronting you while you focus your energy on healing or supporting a loved one.

The amount of financial and legal issues can seem

overwhelming. That is why it is wise to have a plan before experiencing one of life's disruptions. No matter where you find yourself, mid-disruption or looking to plan ahead, the following chapters can help you create a path forward.

# Regaining Control
## with Michael R. Perna

As Nancy and I started to rough out the themes and chapter titles for this book, we originally called this chapter; *I Will Get To It One Day*. For many of us, thinking about a will, health care proxy, or power of attorney fall into the category of once all the important stuff is taken care of, we will get to it. Considering such documents is not always fun, and demands we think about realities most of us would much rather ignore.

Nancy and I invited our attorney, Michael R. Perna, to share his thoughts on what legal documents should be in place. We appreciate the title he gave the chapter, *Regaining Control*. While it may be work to get these documents in place, there is a sense of peace and calm that comes with knowing you have taken steps to protect yourself and your family.

Michael has not only helped Nancy and me, but he has also helped my parents. As mom and dad moved to PA, we visited with Michael to review their plans and ensure everything was in place. Michael helped us see some more significant issues that needed to be addressed. With his help, we made sure mom and dad's estate plan was in good shape. As the years passed and both mom and dad slipped deeper into the darkness of dementia, I cannot tell you how thankful I am that we made time for what were complicated and awkward conversations. While not easy, they ensured that mom and dad received the best care possible.

Listen as Michael helps us understand some simple steps to help us *regain control* of the disruptions that life often brings our way.

When untimely confronted with the prospect of our own mortality, it is only natural to turn inward and dwell upon the "me" questions. Sooner or later, however, our concern shifts to the well-being of those we love. Perhaps we feel we are "leaving them behind" or fear that we are saddling them with unexpected and life-altering emotional, logistical, and financial challenges. Yet, in the haze of these unwelcome events, there are practical measures we can take to alleviate some of the day-to-day burdens on ourselves and our loved ones. Taking these steps can bring some clarity and control to the situation. From a legal standpoint, much can be done to manage what otherwise seems like an unmanageable turn of events.

It is also important to remember that such legal or "estate planning" is no different from what all individuals - even healthy ones – are well-advised to do. In other words, the impending health crisis does not change the need for or process of sound legal planning. On the contrary, it only accelerates it because the crucial questions we must ask ourselves as we embark upon this process are the same for everyone:

- Who is best suited to make medical decisions on my behalf if a time should come when I cannot do so for myself?

- Who should I appoint to handle my financial affairs while I am still living, and what guidelines should I give them?
- Who are the important people in my life, and how can I best provide for them after I am gone?

There are three basic legal documents that can be utilized to implement the answers to the above questions. They are, respectively, a **Health Care Directive** (sometimes loosely referred to as a "Living Will"), a **Power of Attorney**, and a **Last Will and Testament**. The first two documents are used to facilitate the management of our healthcare and financial affairs while we are still living and will terminate on death. At this time, only the Last Will and Testament will govern the payment of debts and the disposition of estate assets.

In tailoring the above three documents to our specific needs and concerns, it is wise to evaluate the background and temperament of those individuals who we select to act on our behalf. One also should consider whether any members of our family or other loved ones have special needs or are too young to responsibly manage the assets we may leave them. If so, a document called a "trust is often the best way to address such special circumstances.

The existence, or prospect, of life insurance also should be considered as an estate planning mechanism. Do we have enough? Can we obtain more? Can we convert term policies to whole-life policies?

For those who own or co-own a small business, much can be done to assure that our eventual withdrawal from the business is as seamless as possible. Important questions to consider include whether we want the business to continue, and if so, who would be best equipped to run it? If not, should the business be sold or simply dissolved? Although the company bylaws may provide a mechanism for implementing these decisions, they can be supplemented with further instructions if necessary.

Of course, the prospect of significant inheritance taxes also may be a concern. Yet, here, too, measures can be taken to reduce, if not eliminate, this potential estate liability. For example, to the extent that there are ample liquid or other assets, it may be desirable during our lifetime to schedule annual tax-exempt "gifts" to children or other family members so as to minimize the ultimate estate tax burden. Although the maximum annual gift tax exclusion is currently $16,000 per person, smaller gifts are permitted, and the amount of each gift may vary from individual to individual.

Finally, to shield the estate from diminishment as a result of medical bills uncovered by insurance, assets may be conveyed during our lifetime directly to, or "in trust for," those individuals who otherwise would receive them at our death. However, doing so effectively requires compliance with specific state and federal laws governing such transactions. This typically necessitates the assistance of a qualified professional.

Collectively, the Health Care Directive, Power of Attorney, Last Will and Testament, together with any trusts, life insurance, gifting schedules, and/or business transition documents, are loosely referred to as an "estate plan." It is always advisable to seek the assistance of an estate planning lawyer or other trusted professional when fashioning such an estate plan.

## QUESTIONS TO GUIDE YOUR LEGAL PLANNING:

- Do you have a Health Care Directive? Do you need help understanding the Health Care Directive?
- Do the necessary people know where your Health Care Directive is stored? For example, do your doctors have a copy? Does the hospital you use have a copy on file?

- Do you have a Power of Attorney? Have you communicated the name of the POA to the necessary family members? Does your POA have a copy of the document?
- Do you have a Last Will and Testament? When was it last updated? Does it reflect the realities of your life today (children, investments, property holdings, etc.)?
- Have you met with an estate planning lawyer to have them review or help you develop your estate plan?
- Do your family members know the name of your lawyer? Do they have contact information for your lawyer?
- Have you met with your lawyer **recently** to ensure everything is in order and you are providing as clear a picture as possible for your loved ones?

# FINANCES

## WITH PAUL MAYNOR

One of the most difficult conversations Nancy and I ever had took place in Paul Maynor's office. Paul is our financial planner and a good friend.

I had been in treatment for a few months, and piled upon the stress of my diagnosis was the question of how we would manage financially. For Nancy, the stress was compounded by her taking care of our finances. Nancy feels a burden to ensure I have the best care possible, and at the same time, is anxious when thinking of trying to live on her own should I pass.

One afternoon we took all that raw emotion and dropped it in the conference room of Paul's office. Sitting around a large table, we talked about the realities of my diagnosis before turning to the issues that brought us there. Paul calmly and confidently poured over our financial reality and helped strategize for the future, whatever that may be.

Nancy fought back tears as she answered questions dealing with life insurance policies, disability payments, and different financial scenarios that felt very threatening.

Leaving Paul's office, we had some answers and a plan for moving forward. Most importantly, Nancy knew that if/when something happened to me, one of the first people she needs to call is Paul. Knowing she would not be left to figure things out on her own gave her a sense of confidence. For me (Dan), the reality that Nancy, Paul, and I have dealt with complex financial questions gives me peace. In addition, the fact that Paul will be there to assist Nancy brings me great comfort.

That initial conversation in Paul's office was scary. It fits into the top three most difficult conversations during our journey. However, having the conversation with someone we trusted allowed us to experience some peace regarding our finances and get about the work of living with cancer. We asked Paul to share some of his wisdom regarding financial planning.

Time. Time is of the essence. Time heals all wounds, time marches on, and time's up!

Many things have been written about this phenomenon we call time. Arguably, it may be your most valuable and precious asset and ally or your most feared enemy and challenge. Yet, it is constant and applies equally to everyone on the planet.

We have the ability to change many things in our lives, our address, our friends, our careers, etc., but we cannot change anything we have already done or what has happened. We cannot go back in time. Don't you wish you had just sixty seconds, ONE MINUTE, of "do-over" time where you can step back just three seconds or so and retract that statement or action??? How much easier would life be if we could correct some errors before they happen?

Sadly, no one possesses the do-over button, so we have to live with the decisions we make today.

In my practice, I see all walks of people. I sit with folks who have diligently saved and have few worries when they transition to retirement, regardless of what the markets bring. I have visited with others who will continue to live paycheck to paycheck well into retirement. These people, all the while best-intentioned, may have to find work after they retire just to make ends meet. The first group saw time as their friend, while the latter ignored it, and now it is their worst adversary.

I believe it is Einstein that termed compound interest as the Eighth Wonder of the World. I have often said that the first million is the hardest; the rest just seem to fall into place. I tell you all of this to stress that there is no one "best" time to start taking care of yourself financially. Actually, there is NOW.

For those of you reading this, if you have chosen to use time as your partner, I commend you. For those of you who have not, let this be the catalyst for change! Decide NOW to start paying yourself first. Yes, pay yourself FIRST. Before you pay your rent, mortgage, AT&T, Verizon, JC Penny, Mastercard, Visa, or Discover, pay YOU. You are more important than all of those companies. If you don't have enough at the end of the month, you have chosen a lifestyle you cannot afford. Even if it is five dollars a week, do it. It may not sound like a lot, but just $20 a month over a thirty-year period at just a 6% rate of return, far less than the markets have returned historically, is more than 30,000 dollars! Imagine if you did even more! The numbers are staggering!

I remember when my daughter got her first job. I sat her down to teach her how money worked and what to do when she got paid. I suggested she emulate my grandfather, Kelso. When he got paid for working at the Goodrich Tire Company in Akron, Ohio, he and my grandmother would walk to the bank to deposit it. They put some in savings and paid everyone else after. He did well for himself and our family and community because of his fiscal discipline.

My first financial planner sat me down years ago and took an objective look at my numbers, and he helped me tremendously. So much so that I entered the industry after I left the Air Force. I have helped many couples and individuals build and design a path to their ultimate financial independence. It may take another set of eyes looking into your books to provide you with the advice you may need.

Take this moment to decide that you WILL ask for an objective opinion on what's going on under your financial roof. An excellent resource is the CFP website to look for someone in your area who, as a fiduciary, will give you the best possible advice, putting your best interests first. Good luck, and I wish you a happy, healthy, and financially secure path!

Let me (Dan) provide some final words to Paul's sharing.

When you are in the midst of a significant life disruption, like the diagnosis of a life-threatening disease or fighting to recover from an accident, it will feel like you have NO TIME. Life seems to speed up and slow down all at the same time.

There will be doctor appointments, treatment plans to follow, and all kinds of arrangements to make. It will feel like there is no time for even the simplest of things, laundry, eating, and relaxing for five minutes.

When moving in a season such as that, it is reasonable for us to say, "when life slows down a little, we will deal with the financial future." I understand. Nancy and I walked that road. We want to encourage you to make the time to address this most important reality of your journey.

It takes time to find a financial advisor (two good ones are listed at the back of this book). It takes time to speak with an advocate at the hospital to see if there is a way they can help your family through this season. You may be exhausted, ask someone to come alongside and help you with the difficult conversations. Maybe a friend, family member, church member, or someone in a club you are a part of. Whatever it takes, make the time. It could lead to new possibilities, peace, and hope amidst your season of chaos.

# INSURANCE

Do you have a life insurance plan? Yes? Do you know the details of your life insurance plan? If not, that is the difference between us.

At 47, my husband was diagnosed with stage four cancer. We were a two-income household. Six months earlier, we bought a new home based on two incomes. Overnight, our future, including our financial future, changed drastically. While my foremost thoughts were about Dan's health, our love, and our future together, there were also fiscal responsibilities that could not be ignored.

In our family, I (Nancy) pay the bills. I am aware of how much money comes in and goes out. It has been my responsibility for years to take our paychecks and make sure our bills were covered. Now, suddenly, I needed more information about what the future would hold for our family financially.

The first time I sat down and read our life insurance policy from beginning to end, I felt so guilty. I was checking to see what money I would receive when Dan died. I felt so guilty. I felt even worse when I told Dan I had read the policy. Dan was glad. He knew we needed to know the details. We needed to know the process.

The act of learning this information literally gave me a headache. But I was glad I had the information. Knowledge is helpful. So many pieces of living with a terminal illness are damaging, but knowing how to overcome those challenges is helpful. Dan knows that if he passes, I will receive financial help that will make life sustainable. Knowledge is good.

I learned that we would receive different amounts of insurance depending on Dan's age at the time of death. (This sounds so cold-hearted even as I write it.) During the final year of a terminal illness, we could pull funds off the life insurance if needed. Armed with this information, we made an appointment with our financial planner. We discussed whether I could afford to stay in our house alone based on the life insurance policy. I had another headache.

Love endures all things, but bills must be paid. We needed to know the details of what was in our life insurance policy. We are blessed to have one. Suppose you answered the first question of this chapter with a no (do you have life insurance). In that case, I advise you to purchase a life insurance policy, if possible. If you have a policy already, read it. Chances are you will find it confusing. This may be an opportunity to ask someone for help. Find someone who can interpret the insurance language and help you understand what you are required to do and what benefits the policy provides.

None of this will be easy. Information is power. Knowledge will provide peace and help you determine a path forward.

## QUESTIONS TO ASK ABOUT LIFE INSURANCE:

- Do you have life insurance? Have you ever taken the time to read your life insurance policy?
- What is the process of filing a claim?
- When can you file the claim? After death only or at an earlier time?

- Does the amount of the insurance payout vary depending on factors such as the age of the insurance holder at the time of death?
- Do you have beneficiaries of the insurance plan filed with the company? Do you know who the beneficiaries are?
- Is there someone in your circle of support that knows where the insurance policy is? You may need help with details such as this at the time of death.

## QUESTIONS TO CONSIDER FOR OTHER TYPES OF INSURANCE RELATED TO HEALTH AND WORK:

- Do you have long-term care (nursing home) insurance?
- What is the maximum payout of any long-term care insurance?
- Do you have long-term disability insurance? Who is the owner of the long-term disability insurance? How do you file a claim?
- Do you know how to file a disability claim with Social Security? Do you know what paperwork you must collect to file a Social Security claim?

## QUESTIONS TO CONSIDER FOR OTHER INSURANCE NOT RELATED TO HEALTH:

- Who is the company that carries your auto insurance? Do you have a contact or phone number?
- Who is the company that carries your home insurance? Do you have a contact or phone number?

- Where is your insurance information with an account number and policy details? Do you have a paper file? If you have online access, where is your login information?

# Preparing To Avoid Chaos Amidst Disruptions
## with John L. Blair

We have spent much time discussing the legal and financial realities facing individuals and families dealing with disruptions in their lives. In my (Dan) opinion, these are some of the most practical yet uncomfortable conversations you can have. Start slowly, and take breaks when one of you needs to step away. Always return to the conversation until you have completed preparing for your future.

We will close this section with some words from John L. Blair. John is the Managing Director of Client Relations for DT Investment Partners. I (Dan) met John after sharing about this book project with a friend. After listening to me share, they said, "You need to talk to John; he is passionate about these issues." So John and I met for coffee, and he shared some of his experiences working with people wrestling with unpacking legal and financial entanglements after losing a loved one. John put the following together to share with his clients. It is an excellent synopsis of what Nancy and I feel is important to talk about.

Over the past few weeks, I have had multiple meetings with clients that have not yet completed their estate documents. I have also, unfortunately, lost a client at the age of 62 and a friend at the age of 56. This seemed like a good time to send a brief note on a topic most do not like to discuss. The emotional stress and sadness from losing a spouse or parent can be devastating. I often see this pain compounded by the fact that difficult discussions around a person's last wishes were avoided until it is too late.

**Estate Documents**: It is recommended that everyone have the three basic estate documents:

1. A **Will** is a legal declaration of the intention of the testator, with respect to his or her property which he or she desires to be carried out after his or her death.

2. **Power of Attorney** (POA) is a legal document giving one person (the agent or attorney-in-fact) the power to act for another person (the principal). The power of attorney is frequently used in the event of a principal's illness or disability or when the principal can't be present to sign necessary documents for financial transactions.

3. **Advanced Healthcare Directives** guide choices for doctors and caregivers if you are terminally ill, seriously injured, in a coma, in the late stages of dementia, or near the end of life.

**Financial Matters:** Keep it simple as possible. People often overcomplicate things with unnecessary trusts and estate planning in order to impose their control after their death.

1. Provide all necessary contact information.

- Investment advisor
- Banks

- Insurance Agent
- Estate Attorney
- CPA / Accountant and location of past tax returns
- Pension payments or cash balance accounts

2. Have a list of all accounts and pertinent information.

- Insurance Policy type and expiration
- Bank accounts: (Bank name, account number, and type of account)
- Investment accounts (Custodian, account number, and type of account)
- IRA or 401k accounts (Custodian and account number)

3. Have a financial plan that accounts for all contingencies. This should include a list of Beneficiaries.

A **letter of Instruction** is a less seldom addressed document but is also very important. Where a Will is the legal document that will transition your estate to your heirs, a letter of instruction assists in the process and provides guidance to your surviving family members or heirs. The letter of instruction can include the following:

1. Location in your home or safe deposit box of Personal papers such as:

- Your Will
- Car Titles (should only be in one name, never owned jointly)
- Deeds
- Insurance Policies
- Funeral Information
- Care of Pets, primarily for single people

2. Personal guidance to your heirs to assist them in moving forward:

- Whom to trust to assist with decisions. Suggestions as to when to meet and the goals of the meeting.
- Guidance on how money should be invested going forward, allocation to stocks, bonds, C/D's, and cash.
- How to structure income distributions going forward.
- What to do with Life Insurance proceeds – Pay off debt, invest, or keep in cash.
- Give them the freedom to do what they need to do without pressure. You trust them!
- Your guidance as to which automobiles should be kept or sold.
- Your guidance regarding keeping real estate, primary home, and vacation homes.

These are difficult conversations on a topic most like to avoid. However, once it is done, you will have greater peace of mind, and when the time comes, you will save your heir(s) additional stress and concern.

# CAN FEAR BE MY FRIEND?

While fear had always been an acquaintance of mine, lately, it seems to be my shadow. In the past, many of my fears (or phobias as my family called them) were not probable but more the product of an overactive imagination: what if the roller coaster crashes while I am on the top; what if the last person who read this library book had a contagious disease; what if an escaped prisoner breaks into my house the one night of the year Dan is out of town? Not fears that have come true.

## REALISTIC FEARS

Today, my fears are more realistic. What if Dan catches an illness during Chemotherapy and can't recover? What if the tumors start growing again? Can I pay the mortgage if we go down to one income? Am I giving our children enough attention, or will they grow to resent me? Like fears of the past, these may also not come to fruition, but there is a thin line between ignoring fears and planning to overcome possible problems.

There are days that I wake up and greet the day as a new

opportunity. But, on other days, I seem to make a constant mental list of all the new fears in my life. Thinking about fears makes me wonder if I am worrying, which shows a lack of faith and makes me afraid I am even letting God down in my weakness. But on the other hand, ignoring these issues could be reckless because then I won't be ready to face them if they become real.

## GETTING FRIENDLY WITH OUR FEARS

As I was driving one day, I felt as if my list of fears was harassing me and making me miserable. I thought of another time in my life when there were people in my life that seemed to be harassing me and making me miserable. After giving in to them didn't work and ignoring them was useless, I tried becoming friendly with them and seeing if good could come from the relationship. Sometimes it worked, and years later, I realized that having that difficult period of life made me who I am today.

Can fear be my friend and make me a better person? The more I considered the idea, I found it held promise.

Facing my fears can lead me to develop relationships. For example, fears related to Dan's sickness and our future have led to many conversations. We have discussed everything from disability insurance to life insurance to planning a trip to Roatan when Dan is healthy enough. We have begun to problem-solve how to meet our challenges while also sharing dreams and private thoughts. I have also talked to others about my fears where I would not have shared with them or understood their viewpoint if I had not been afraid.

My fears have led me to get to know myself better. I have had to reach into depths that have not been tapped before. I have helped in areas that, in the past, would have been Dan's domain. I have learned to plug along even when tired. While self-reliance has never been a goal, I am learning that it is not out of reach.

## A STEP AWAY FROM WORRY

Fear has brought me closer to God. My current relationship with God ranges from quiet moments to moments of despair and tears. There are times when I am content with God's direction for my life and times when I am not on God's side. Fear has not pushed me away from God but keeps pushing me to God because I know I can't make it alone. Going to God with my fear holds me a step away from worry and allows me to understand, "Come unto me all who are weary, and I will give you rest," in a new light.

Fear is putting life in focus. Realizing I don't have to falter and fail under fear, but instead, I can go to God, others, and even myself to face the fear, I find that there are fewer surprises. I am beginning to see the pitfalls around me and keep going. There are days I want to allow fear to cripple me, but I am learning instead to make it my friend.

## OVERWHELMING FEARS...BUT GOD

When I was in Roatan this summer, a dog walked up and licked my leg. I had heard a story once about the child of a missionary being licked by a dog and dying from rabies. I immediately began to panic because my family needs me, and I don't like shots. (Fears sometimes come in doubles.) The first friend I told about the lick told me to wipe my leg off and gave me the "Are you crazy?" look. The second (a doctor) told me I had bigger worries in my life than being licked by a dog. When I returned home rabies free, I realized I had reached out to others and spent time in prayer. It may have been a crazy fear, but in the end, all was good.

Life can be overwhelming. Fears can be real. But God is good all the time. If fear becomes my friend, even my fears can remind me that all the time, God is good. [1]

# PART THREE
# DAY-TO-DAY REALITIES

When disruptions strike, our focus naturally shifts towards the urgent and sustaining a sense of normalcy in our life. There are many things we take for granted, things that "just happen" and exist quietly in our lives. We take them for granted until, suddenly, a disruption causes us to figure out a new way to deal with them.

This chapter highlights a few places that we tend to take for granted yet are worthy of our attention. A little time in planning and preparing will allow these everyday realities to continue without much disruption.

Nancy and I are confident that as we share a few here, you will think of many more within your life.

# Navigating the Healthcare System

W hile it is true that not all of life's disruptions are caused by illness, many require learning to navigate the modern healthcare system.

In the seven years that Nancy and I have been navigating our country's healthcare system, we have noticed significant changes. Changes have required us to rethink how we interact with doctors and nurses.

## Healthcare Portals

The most significant change has been an increased reliance on healthcare portals for communication and care. Close to one hundred percent of my appointments are scheduled and communicated via the health care portal. Before every appointment, I am expected to login to the portal and complete a pre-appointment check-in. For many of us, this has become the new normal for communicating with those who care for us.

I love the ease with which I can reach out to the doctors on my care team. Using the portal, I can send a quick message and get a response in just a few hours. For non-urgent or routine concerns, this is a perfect way to streamline communication. However, it is less helpful when there is a pressing issue.

On one occasion, I was working on scheduling a rather urgent procedure. The stent in my liver was backed up, and if left unaddressed, I was headed toward liver failure. When this happens, I have zero energy and sleep most of the day. I used the portal to contact the GI team, who would do my procedure. Once done, I went to bed and slept for seven hours. When I looked at the portal to see their reply message, the office was closed for the day. Using the portal, we managed to make arrangements the following day. A simple phone call would have made communication much more straightforward.

This should not be a big issue if you are tech-savvy and easily navigate things like healthcare portals. However, should you be one of those people who do not move well within the world of healthcare portals, this could be an excellent opportunity to ask someone for help. Chances are good you have a child or grandchild who finds this cyber world much easier to navigate. Inviting them to help would give them a very tangible way to help you through your disruption.

## COVID-19 IMPACTS

I (Dan) was hospitalized in early March 2020 as COVID upended our world. My room was feet away from the nursing station. At each shift change, there were new protocols and procedures for the nursing staff to adapt to. Gone were the relaxed conversations about family and time away from work. Instead, everything had a sense of urgency.

Changes were made in the name of patient safety. Of all those changes, the most impactful to Nancy and me was that no visitors were allowed. Where we used to navigate hospitalizations together, I was alone, and Nancy felt in the dark about what was going on. While some visitation restrictions have been relaxed, Nancy is still not allowed to stay the night like she was pre-covid.

We have noticed several changes from the height of the COVID pandemic, which are still in place within the healthcare system. You will most likely notice changes if you have not actively navigated the hospital systems since COVID.

## The Importance of Advocacy

Successfully navigating the modern healthcare system demands you learn to advocate for yourself. We are blessed with doctors and nurses who do their best to care for us. The depth of their knowledge and the resources at their disposal is like nothing our world has ever seen. Yet they are pulled in two competing directions. They have dedicated themselves to caring for their patients. It is their calling. At the same time, the insurance system within which they work demands they see an ever-growing number of patients each day. There have been studies done that speak to the amount of time patients actually spend with their doctors.

*Average length of visits was 17.4 minutes. The median length of visits was 15.7 minutes. The median talk time by patient was 5.3 minutes, and physician, 5.2 minutes.* [1]

*A 1999 study of 29 family physician practices found that doctors let patients speak for only 23 seconds before redirecting them; Only one in four patients got to finish his or her statement.* [2]

You will need an advocate to get the care you or your loved one needs within this kind of system. Someone to speak for you and to push to ensure you get the quality care you deserve. It can very well be a matter of life or death.

During one of my most significant hospital stays, we were struggling to understand and address the damage that had been done to my liver. One of my cancer treatments had a three percent chance of damaging the bile ducts in my liver. Unfortunately, I happened to fall in that three percent. Doctor after doctor came into my hospital room, and each shared a different story. "We can fix this; there will be no lasting side effects." "We might be able to address the issue, but there is lasting damage." "I am sorry, there is nothing we can do, your liver is destroyed, and you cannot survive without a liver." Each one shared their opinion and then left. It was one massive rollercoaster ride.

During one conversation, I had three doctors from the GI team discussing different options, each advocating for a slightly different treatment plan. At one point, I asked them to be quiet for a moment and let me make a phone call. I called my primary oncologist (I have his cell number – yes, he is that kind of a guy, which is why I love him). After Dr. Saroha and I finished discussing the options, I turned back to the doctors in the room and told them what we would be doing. One doctor looked at me with their mouth on the floor and demanded to know who I had just spoken to. I smiled and said, "The oncologist who has kept me alive for the past four years, so his opinion matters." That interaction, while not easy, reset my relationship with those doctors. We worked together differently from that time forward.

We moved forward with the plan. The GI team successfully completed an ERCP, allowing my bile ducts to flow freely and moving me away from liver failure. However, in the days following that initial procedure, we were told I could only have a couple of ERCPs. They were risky, and that GI team insisted that it was not a procedure that could be done more than once or twice. We had challenging conversations about what would happen if and when my bile ducts became backed up again. They were extraordinarily compassionate but said there was only so much they could do to help me.

Nancy and I kept asking, prodding, and pushing until I ended up with a GI doctor specializing in my area of need. At the time I am writing this, I have just completed my twelfth ERCP. Dr. Leung is comfortable doing them as needed, which has worked out to be every two months. I am haunted by those earlier conversations where I was told the ERCP was something we could do a limited number of times. Each time I see Dr. Leung, I ask, "You are okay continuing to do these ERCPs?" He always smiles and says we know the risks, but we also know I need it to survive. Had Nancy and I listened to the first opinion we were given, my family would have gathered for my memorial service years ago.

Advocacy is important. You need to advocate for yourself or find someone who will speak on your behalf. If you are uncomfortable pushing back and asking questions, find someone who can do it for you. Learn to ask why and whether there are other options. Seek a second opinion before undergoing a procedure. It makes sense. Most of us find it reasonable and prudent to get multiple quotes (opinions) before undergoing a renovation project at home. So why do we struggle to do the same regarding our bodies and healthcare?

## WE HAVE ADVOCATES WITHIN THE SYSTEM

Nancy and I have learned over the years that most healthcare systems have done an excellent job of building patient advocates into their systems. However, they are often some of the best-kept secrets within a healthcare system. As a patient, the challenge will be to find and build a relationship with them.

The easiest way to find help is to ask. Sometimes the best person to ask might be the office receptionist. Do not be afraid to express your need and see if someone in the system might be able to help you. Often these people are referred to as *Patient Advocates*. In larger systems, each patient advocate may have an area of expertise (finances, drug co-pays, arranging appointments). The key is to know that these people exist and keep asking until you get the help you need. Checking in with a patient advocate regularly is wise if your disruption means a long season of navigating the healthcare system.

Nancy was talking to one of my patient advocates about an unrelated issue when they asked, "Have you ever applied for financial assistance with your co-pays?" We had not, and Nancy said we would continue to work on our payment plan. However, the patient advocate insisted we apply. Ultimately, the healthcare system we work with forgave a significant amount of medical debt for us. None of that would have happened without speaking to a patient advocate.

## A FINAL THOUGHT

Whenever I encounter a situation that requires me to advocate for myself or navigate a new system such as the healthcare portal, I think about my parents. Mom and dad grew up in an era where you believed what the doctors said and accepted their words as truth. Pushing back or advocating for a different opinion or second option was beyond their comprehension. Navigating new technology meant they were left behind. They needed someone to advocate for them. Although mom and dad had healthcare portals, they have never seen them. As the power of attorney, Nancy and I manage that for them. We joined them at doctor appointments so we could hear what was said and ask questions when needed.

I am convinced many people do not receive the healthcare they need or deserve because they lack a voice to speak on their behalf. Who in your world needs an advocate? How might you help them find one?

## QUESTIONS TO HELP THINK ABOUT ADVOCACY:

- Does the caregiver (or someone) have access to the healthcare portal of the patient to help understand the correspondence on the portal?
- Is there a list available to the patient and caregiver of the current doctors involved in medical care and their contact information?
- Have you identified challenging areas so you can find help: understanding medical information, locating the best doctors, finding the locations for testing, understanding billing, and making payments?
- Are there others in your network of friends and family that have had a similar experience with a medical condition? Can that person be of assistance as you work to understand the medical situation?
- If the caregiver or patient finds it difficult to advocate for the patient with the medical team, who can you ask to help with medical visits and phone calls to better advocate for the best possible care?
- Is there an advocate or social worker available from the doctor's office? If so, do you have the contact information so you can begin a conversation?

# Technology / Social Media

It might be my age (fifty-five), but it feels like each day, a new app or service is supposed to make my life easier. I am not sure that any of it actually improves my life, but it certainly gives me one more thing to keep track of.

The sneaky thing about such services and apps is that they become a part of our life, and we slowly forget they exist. We take them for granted and assume they will be there and continue working. But, unfortunately, our technology needs to be cared for.

One often overlooked part of legacy planning is providing a way for your loved ones to access the apps and services that store so much of your important information.

Take a moment and think about all the passwords you have. How often do you change or update them? Do you update a record of the passwords, or do you rely upon the fact that you can reset most passwords? Does anyone other than you have access to your passwords? For most of our lives we are encouraged to keep such information private. Should something happen to you, my guess is that your heirs would find access to some apps or services helpful.

What if someone needed to cancel a service or app? How would they go about it?

There are a myriad of different services or apps (no surprise) that can safely protect your passwords and allow you to share them with a few trusted family members. However you choose to do it, we recommend you find a way to start recording the multiple pieces of login information for the apps and services you use.

Some services provide legacy or memorialization settings. These go largely unnoticed. It takes only a few minutes to set them up. Doing so provides loved one's access and control of online information that could otherwise be lost. Here are just two examples.

**Google Inactive Account Manager**: You can set up a plan for what happens to your Google account when you are no longer able to access it. As of publication, Google allows you to set different inactivity periods that trigger Google reaching out to trusted contacts you identify. In addition, you can arrange different levels of access for each contact. One thing to keep in mind is that the contacts you identify to receive access to your account cannot change their email and phone number between the time you set this up and when they will need access. I (Dan) provided three trusted contacts in hopes that one will have the same contact information when it is needed.

Visit https://myaccount.google.com/inactive for more details and to set up your Google inactive account manager plan.

**Facebook:** Under memorialization settings, Facebook allows you to set a legacy contact. Doing a Google search for Facebook Memorialization Settings, Legacy Contact will provide you with step-by-step instructions on how to do so.

> *If Facebook is made aware that a person has passed away, it's our policy to memorialize the account. Memorialized accounts are a place for friends and family to gather and share memories after a person has passed away. Memorializing an account also helps keep it secure by preventing anyone from logging into it.*

> *If you're a legacy contact, learn how to manage a memorialized account. If you'd like to report a deceased person's account to be memorialized, please contact us.* [1]

Many apps and services you use will do something similar.

## Why is this important

With everything that must be addressed, legacy planning for our technology can easily seem something best left for another day. It would be easy to focus on other things. Let me share with you why this is so important.

I (Dan) use a program named Evernote to help plan and prepare for my eventual death. Evernote lets me create notebooks and folders to store all kinds of information. Then, you can easily search the folders to find information. I plan to provide Nancy with everything she needs when caring for our home and vehicles within Evernote. I attempted to find some form of legacy setting within Evernote. Instead, I found they were very protective of my privacy and data (something I am thankful for).

*Evernote's pledge to protect the privacy of your Content **will continue, even after your death or incapacity.** If you wish to enable someone to have access to your Content or other data in your account after you are no longer able to provide them access, you need to implement a process for providing your information to them. **We will not provide your information, or your Content, to anyone, even next of kin, unless we determine that we are legally obligated to do so.** We encourage you to include your Basic Subscriber information, with instructions on how to access your Content, in your will or other estate plans, so that anyone you wish to have access to your account will have the means to do so. Please see our Commercial Terms for information on terminating payment for Paid Services upon death or incapacity.* [2] *(emphasis mine)*

Evernote requires you to make plans for someone else to access your data. Information like this might be something to include in the "letter of instruction" that John talked about in the previous chapter. However you handle it, recognize that some tech companies will not assist your loved ones in gaining access to your data and accounts. Instead, they work hard to protect your privacy, even after death. Navigating this reality well will require planning.

## STEPS TO SECURING YOUR TECHNOLOGY AND SOCIAL MEDIA:

- Eliminate services or apps you no longer need or use.
- Make a list of all services and apps you use. One way to do this is to look at all the passwords saved by your web browser. For example, Google automatically saves login information for you, how would someone else access that website or program on your behalf? How do you

plan to communicate this information to those needing it in the future?

- Provide complete login information for each service.
- Find a safe way to store login information. There are services that encrypt the data for you.
- Do you have a system to keep that list of login information up to date as you change passwords? (*This is important for people like Nancy who use the "lost password" feature on a regular basis.*)
- Which services will assist your loved ones in gaining access to necessary data? Do any of these services resist sharing in order to protect your privacy? Are there steps you can take to make the process easier for your loved ones?
- Do you want to include information about passwords and technology in your legacy planning with a lawyer or financial planner?

# VEHICLES

I (Dan) have largely viewed our automobiles as tools that helped us get from point A to point B. Nancy and I tend to purchase a vehicle and then run it until it "hollers mercy" and throws up a white flag of surrender.

For others, an automobile is much more. We have family members who I am honestly afraid to ride with. I fear they love their car more than me. If I was to accidentally close the door too hard or leave a mark somewhere, I am confident I would be left alongside the road.

Chances are good you identified which category you fall into as you read this. Wherever you fall, our automobiles are one of life's major purchases. Leaving instructions, or at least providing direction for family members, can help as they navigate seasons of disruption.

Suppose you have spent a lifetime collecting and restoring the vehicles you drive. In that case, your loved ones may feel compelled to hold on to vehicles they do not know how to maintain. Worse yet, there may be "discussions" about who should end up with what vehicle. Again, providing guidance can help avoid hurt feelings.

## SOME QUESTIONS TO THINK ABOUT REGARDING VEHICLES:

- Make a list of the vehicles you own. Where will people find the titles? If payments are due, what bank, when are payments due, and how much do you owe?
- Are vehicles registered in your name? Do family members understand the process of re-registering vehicles under a different name? Is this something that you could do now?
- Do you have a pre-paid service plan or warranty on repairs for your vehicle? Where are the details located?
- Do you have guidance regarding what happens to specific vehicles after you pass away? Is it clearly written down? Where? Who has the document?
- Are there special stories about the history of your vehicles that are important to you? Have you communicated those? Who will pass along those stories? [for example, I once owned a 74 Chevy Nova that used to be my grandmother's. That history was important. It made the car special. There were stories about how my grandfather purchased it for her that made it even more special.

# WHERE CAN IT BE?

When our children were young, I (Nancy) created the brown striped notebook. There was a section with our life insurance policy, medical and school information for each child, and other important information. As our children got old enough to understand, they had the direction that if something happened to Dan and me, they were to take the brown striped notebook to Uncle Rob. Rayann and Joseph did not understand the significance of the notebook. They just had their marching orders. The notebook held enough information to get someone started in caring for our children, and Uncle Rob had the background to know who needed what information.

As our children became young adults, I stopped worrying about needing someone to care for them. Now, however, there is a new urgency. I may need to produce the health care proxy or power of attorney paperwork if Dan goes into a medical crisis. If something happens to Dan, I become the caretaker of his parents, needing to know how Dan takes care of their bills and needs. Organization matters more than a list in my brain of what I believe is in our safety deposit box at the bank.

Another issue beyond my knowledge is knowing that if Dan is at the end of his life, I imagine I will not be functioning at the highest level of memory and reasoning. In addition, at that point in time, someone else may need to find documents or access important information for me. So, sharing this information with a trusted friend or family member also becomes important.

Another reason organization becomes critical. We have a safety deposit box at the bank, and I generally know what is in it. That is an OK system for regular life. But in a crisis, there needs to be more clarification on finding the power of attorney, vehicle title, or other important documents. When dealing with a crisis, not finding the correct paperwork easily creates another, more emotional crisis. To prevent this, I need to reinstate a newer version of the brown-striped notebook. There needs to be a central system of organization so that important documents can be found. Easily. Quickly.

## DOCUMENTS YOU NEED TO BE ABLE TO LOCATE QUICKLY AND EASILY:

- Identification documents: Birth certificate, driver's license or state photo ID, passport, Social Security cards.
- Marriage license.
- Will, Power of Attorney, and Health Care Proxy (if you do not have any of these, you may want to see a lawyer).
- Health Insurance card(s).
- Titles for vehicles.
- Home mortgage or ownership information.
- List all bank accounts, Investment information, or your financial advisor's name.
- Military service records.

- Education information.
- Name of supervisor at work and their phone number.
- Name of insurance company (auto, home, life, disability).
- List of primary doctors (with contact information).

# SILENT TEARS

Awake at 3 a.m., mind full of dread as we enter back into the valley
of the shadow of death
My fear is real as I lay still and try not to share my emotion
**Instead, without a sound, I cry silent tears.**

Earlier in the day, as the doctor walked in with a frown and began
to describe the next wave
I began to envision what was coming down the path
**Trying to be calm, inside I shed silent tears.**

Sharing information with family and friends is a delicate balance of
relaying facts while also
Trying to portray a feeling of hope, even if unsure
**So, I try to sound cheerful and hide the silent tears.**

During church, as life goes on normally around me and I try to
converse and be myself,
I want to shout out that nothing is OK right now
**But instead, I smile past my silent tears.**

On the outside, I can work and take care of my family and shop
and talk and smile
But my mind strays even as I try to keep my focus
**Off our troubles to avoid the silent tears.**

Time will heal, and a diagnosis may change. My tears will dry up,
and my life may go on.
But as I look around me, I hope I start to be aware
**Of who else is experiencing silent tears.**[1]

© Nancy Nicewonger 2018

# PART FOUR
# HOME SWEET HOME

Whether a renter or homeowner, the space we call home is ours. We invest a lot of time, energy, and financial capital into turning a building into a home.

Your home's history and maintenance requirements are essential information. The ability to answer simple questions about your home will make living there easier. Making sure everyone can provide answers to these questions is important.

The following chapters help you begin to have caring conversations about your home.

# HOME HISTORY

## WITH CHRISTINA REID

History is important. Those who cannot remember the past are condemned to repeat it. It was George Santayana, in his book *Reason in Common Sense*, who gave us that great quote about the importance of remembering history. Understanding history allows us to appreciate what was and, more significantly, allows us to build for the future. Without understanding what was, it is hard to build for tomorrow.

Relationships have history. Can you imagine trying to build a healthy relationship without understanding your past or the past of your partner? Why are doctors always asking for your health history? It is impossible to treat you today without fully understanding what your body has been through in the past. Everything has a history. The better we understand history, the more efficiently and effectively we can navigate the future.

Your home is no different. Your residence has a history. Depending on how you divide labor responsibilities in your household and who is ill, it might be time for a history lesson.

These historical details might seem like trivia now, but they will be essential information for the future. For example, if you go to make repairs to your home, any good contractor will want some of this information. Likewise, if you make the decision to place your home on the market, a realtor will be asking many of these questions. None of these things are easy to think about right now, but it is vital to get historical details so you can move into the future well.

One of the things I did for Nancy was take a permanent marker and write the installation year on all the mechanical systems in our home. It did not take long and actually helped me when talking with service people. There was no question as to when the water heater, water filtration system, or HVAC system was installed. This simple step would go a long way in making your home history a matter of public record.

I asked my friend, Christina Reid, a realtor with RE/MAX Town & Country, to help with the list of questions in this section. I asked her to provide us with a list of all the things she wished her clients always knew.

## OUR HOMES HISTORY:

## HEATING / COOLING:

- What fuel(s) do you use to heat your home? (electric, gas, oil, propane, wood, solar, other).
- What type of heating system(s) does your home have? (forced hot air, hot water, heat pump, electric baseboard, radiant, etc.).
- Do you have a wood, pellet, or coal stove? Where? Who cleans the chimney (liner) prior to each season?
- How many heating zones are in your home?
- Who services each heating system within your home?

- Do you have a fireplace? Is it working? When was the chimney last cleaned?
- When were heating systems installed?
- Does the home have central air, wall units, or window units?
- If window units, where are they stored during the off-season?
- When was the A/C system(s) installed?

## GENERAL:

- When was the last roof put on?
- Do you have an invisible fence? Is there a drawing of where it goes?
- Does your home have Stucco? Every two years, someone should be caulking around any penetrations into the house (windows, sliders, water fixtures, lights, utility boxes, etc.).
- Is there anywhere in the home that has water issues? How often do you check for issues?
- Does your home have a sump pump? Where? Who services it? When was it last serviced?
- Do you have a pest control company? How often do they come? Is there a contract?

## WARRANTIES:

- Does your home have any warranties/insurance for repairs?
- Does your home have a warranty on windows?

## ELECTRICAL:

- Where is your breaker box located?
- Is your breaker box clearly labeled?
- When was the breaker box last upgraded?
- Does the electrical system use fuses or breakers?
- Is the electrical system solar-powered?
- Do you have a generator? How do you start it? Are there written instructions?

## SEWAGE SYSTEM:

- Is your sewage system public, community (non-public), or private (septic tank)?
- How many tanks does the system have if there is a septic system? Where is the drain field? How many lines are in the drain field? Does your septic system have a pump?
- When were the septic tanks last pumped (cleaned out)?
- Who pumped out the tanks?

## WATER:

- What is your water source: public, well, or other?
- What is the depth of the well?
- When was the well pump last replaced?
- When was the well tank last replaced?
- Where is the water shut off for the entire house?
- Where is the water shut off for the water line to the fridge?

## LANDSCAPING:

- Who will take care of the lawn care, mulch, etc.? Think through the cost of a mower, annual maintenance, gas, and time – unless this is something you enjoy, hiring someone to do it for you might be cheaper.
- Who will take care of snow removal? Does any contract include salting before or after ice storms?

## PLUMBING:

- What plumbing materials are in your home, Copper, Galvanized, PVC, PEX, or other?
- When were the water lines last replaced?
- How do you heat your water? (electric, gas, oil, propane).
- How many water heaters are there? Where are they?
- What type of water heater: tank/tankless? When were they installed?

## WASHER & DRYER:

- Where is the water shut-off for the washer?
- Who is the repair person you use for appliances?
- When were the units purchased? Is there a warranty?

## SECURITY SYSTEMS:

- How many smoke detectors are in your home? Where? When were the batteries last changed? If they do not have replaceable batteries, when were they purchased?

- Are there any in-home sprinklers? Are the fire alarms directly connected to a security system or a local fire department?
- How many carbon dioxide detectors? Where? When were the batteries last changed?
- Does your home have a security system? Where are the company contract and contact information?

## OUTDOOR SPRINKLERS:

- Where is the control box for the outdoor sprinkler system? Where is the water shut-off for the outdoor sprinkler system? Who services the system?

## POOLS / SPAS:

- If you have a pool, what chemicals do you use? Where do you take the water to be tested?
- Is the pool saltwater or chlorine?
- If heated, what is the heat source?
- Any specific instructions regarding opening or closing with seasons?
- Where is the pump located?

## WINDOWS:

- When were the windows installed?
- Is there a warranty on the windows still in effect?

# GENERAL
# MAINTENANCE

Maintenance of any kind is rarely fun or sexy. But, it is the kind of work that "must get done" so we can move on to the business of enjoying life. I (Dan) find that people tend to approach general maintenance in one of two ways:

1. Some people feel routine maintenance is extremely important. They often require everyone around them to display equal dedication to completing all maintenance tasks.
2. Others work from a "run it till it breaks" mindset. As a result, they often refuse to do even the simplest things to ensure equipment remains in good working order.

As we start talking about home maintenance, it is essential to understand which of these two approaches you tend to have. How about the caregiver or care receiver you are walking alongside? How do they view home maintenance? Healthy conversations about what feels like mundane topics will be facilitated by trying to understand how the person you are talking with is experiencing the conversation. It is not easy, but you can do this.

Understanding what and when maintenance needs to be performed on your property is important. More than knowing what, you will need to know the when and where of home maintenance. For example, it does you little good to know your home has a water filtration system if you do not know when or where to change the filters.

During the first year of our marriage, Dan and I went grocery shopping together, paid bills, and cleaned the house together. Then, for the other thirty-one years, we began to compartmentalize tasks. I (Nancy) generally cook, clean, shop, and pay the bills. Dan did home maintenance and renovation. He handled mowing and landscape jobs. Now that he is retired, Dan is in charge of laundry. I can rake leaves and trim the shrubs. Together, we got the jobs done. Together. When there are two of us.

After Dan became sick, two issues came into play. First, Dan no longer had the energy and strength to do all the jobs around the house. Second, he quickly realized that he would take a lot of knowledge of what needed to get done around the house with him if he passed away. As a result, I would be left here with little knowledge.

So, we set out to remedy both issues. I pitched in more as Dan completed tasks around the house. As I helped, he taught me why I was doing something when it had to be done next and the critical steps to remember. Valves now have labels. We have a whiteboard in the furnace room to record the times he has changed water filters and added salt to the water softening system. There is a notebook with directions for resetting specific systems after a power outage.

We have practice sessions. Dan no longer turns off the well when we leave for vacation but watches my daughter or me do it. Smoke detectors have "replace in [year]" written on them. I know where the files are for major appliances. Dan is leaving information behind so I can know how to care for our house if he is no longer here.

## QUESTIONS TO ASK ABOUT THE GENERAL UPKEEP OF THE HOUSE:

- Where are the shut-off valves for the water? Where would you go to shut off the water for the house if there was a leak?
- What company services the HVAC system? What size air filter does the system use? How often do you change it? Where is the filter(s) located?
- Where is the dryer vent to the outdoors? How often does it need to be cleaned?
- Where are the shutoffs for outdoor water spigots located? [hint, there should be indoor shutoffs].
- Does your home have water filters? If so, where are they located, where do you get replacement filters, and how often should they be changed?
- How many smoke detectors does your home have? Where are they located? Do they use batteries? When were the batteries last changed?
- How many carbon dioxide detectors does your home have? Where are they located? Do they use batteries? When were the batteries last changed?
- Does your home have a septic tank(s)? Where is the access cover(s) located? When was the tank(s) last cleaned out?
- Who are your internet, phone, and television provider(s)? Where does any cable(s) enter the house? Where are any routers or other devices located? What passwords do you need to access them?

- Do you have a chimney? Do you use it? When was it last cleaned? Who cleans it for you?
- How does your garbage get picked up? What company is responsible? When does the bill need to get paid?
- Service People: What companies do you prefer to use for your repairs? Is there a tree service you have used in the past?
- Contractors: Is there a general contractor you have built a relationship with? Someone who should be your "go-to person" for emergency repairs?
- Appliance Manuals: Do you keep the service manuals for all your appliances? Where are they? Is there a company you use to service each appliance? It might be helpful to write the service company name and contact information on each service manual, along with the purchase date of the appliance.

# CAN I LIVE HERE ALONE?

Moving to Pennsylvania in 2014 was our sixth relocation as a couple. With this transition, we took over a year to find a home we wanted to purchase. We were looking for a home that would serve us well into retirement. We wanted room for three people now, but big enough for our children to visit with their families of the future. Finally, we found a ranch-style house beautifully set at the top of a steep hill in a quiet, rural area. There is a neighbor on one side and the edge of a forest on two sides.

This home was an excellent fit for our coming years together. However, six months after we moved there, we realized our forever life might not be together. I (Nancy) may be living here alone. That would still seem reasonable unless you know the inner workings of my being.

I am fifty-four years old, and I can't sleep in a house alone. Especially one set off alone in the woods.

There were snake skins in the shed the first year we lived here. So now, when I get a tool out of the shed, I knock on the door and wait for the snakes to hide.

We bought the house based on two working adults. Now we have had years of medical bills, and Dan is on disability.

And the latest obstacle to living alone: Our house sits at the top of a steep hill with a beautiful view. I cannot roll the garbage containers down to the end of the drive for trash pickup. The hill is too steep. And that is at the age of fifty-four. I don't see this getting better with age.

Living alone in the house is not a regular topic of conversation. However, it does come up from time to time. Dan's goal is that I will have the option of staying here if I choose. Since moving in, we have worked on the outdoor gardens, which are a source of peace and joy. Our home is located reasonably close to all facets of our life. I am near the train station when I need to go to the office in Philadelphia. Other than the problems caused by living alone, this would be a great location to remain in.

As a caregiver, I talk with women who have gone through the death of a spouse. Many older women who find themselves alone are often faced with others, including their children, who have opinions and solutions for how they should live. I want to work through these issues with Dan rather than my children feeling the need to make decisions for me.

We received a package in the mail a few weeks after announcing to Dan (out of nowhere) that I could not live in this house alone because of trash troubles. Dan had ordered a gadget that connects to our lawn mower and will also work with a trailer hitch on a car. You hook the trash can to this gadget and pull it down the hill with the lawn mower. My garbage issues will be solved once I become competent at driving our zero-turn lawn mower. [Dan here, the "gadget" is from Garbage Commander, available at www.garbagecommander.com. The first day I reviewed this chapter, Nancy was out on the zero-turn. She did very well.]

As issues present themselves, there are some we can make more manageable on our own. For example, we are considering researching security systems. There are practical ways to ensure that I can stay here when I am alone. Will I decide staying in our home is best for me? I don't know how to predict my feelings in the future. But we are thinking of ways to allow for options.

## QUESTIONS TO CONSIDER WHEN FACED WITH LIVING ALONE:

- Who will make major decisions about how I live after the disruption: I will, on my own; I will, along with my children or others; my children or others will decide for me.
- What will finances allow after the death of my loved one/partner?
- How can I cut back and change my lifestyle when living alone? Cable, internet, food, etc.?
- How will I handle regular tasks such as mowing and snow plowing?
- Who can I call for a crisis (i.e., there is a snake in my shed)?
- Who could walk through my property once a year and help me troubleshoot upcoming work that needs to be done?
- Do I need a security system?
- Do I need an emergency call system in case I get hurt?
- How close is my support system? Will I be isolated living here alone?
- What will my social life look like? Will I be willing to eat out alone?

# WHAT IS STRENGTH?

**What is strength?**
My husband has cancer. Life is hard.
People call me strong. I don't feel strong.

**I feel empty.**
But conversations with friends and shared stories begin to fill the void.

**I lack words.**
But then I sit next to him quietly. Together, in silence, we can recharge.

**I feel helpless.**
But we can rely on the wisdom of the doctors to know how to proceed.

**I see darkness ahead.**
But then we spend precious time together, and I begin to embrace hope.

**I feel torn.**
But then I take a breath and do the best I can for all those who need me at this moment.

**I grieve loss.**
But then I remember that the present is here. We can make the most of now.

**I feel frustration.**
But then I accept people for who they are and the limitations of their emotions.

**I accept truth.**
And live with faith in gratitude for the blessings we have had.

**I feel empathy.**
And share with others going through similar pain.

**I give myself.**
And approach each day of this journey as one I will not regret.

**I feel joy.**
And know that our love will not end but morph into an everlasting bond.

**I stay here.**
And hold his hand and his heart. And am glad that he "can't do this without me."

**What is strength?**
I am not sure. And please stop telling me I have it. But I will keep aiming high.[1]

© Nancy Nicewonger 2020

# Part Five
# End-Of-Life Issues

When time is short, everything takes on a sense of urgency that did not exist days or weeks before. Urgency often creates anxiety. We wrestle with questions of "what if," "if only," and "how will I (we)."

One of our challenges is that we do not walk this season alone. Everyone around us is experiencing the disruption in their unique way. Our emotions are not their emotions, and people rarely process seasons of anxiety in totally compatible and supportive ways.

In the following chapters, we talk about navigating this season well. In addition, there are things we can do to help ourselves, and others find peace and joy amidst a difficult time.

# MAKING THE MOST OF YOUR TIME

L ife's disruptions can indeed introduce stress and anxiety into our world. Yet, in a strange way, they can also lead to us living the best moments of our lives.

I have heard many cancer patients say that while they would gladly give up the disease, they are grateful for the lessons learned while on the journey. It sounds strange, but I have found it to be true in my own life.

My disruption gave me greater clarity about what was important in life. At the same time, I gained the ability to say "no" like never before. With limited energy and a sense of limited time, I was only willing to invest in those things most important to me. As a result, I found myself speaking with greater clarity and sharing my expectations without apology. The goal was to make the most of whatever time I had left. As it turns out, I have had much more time than doctors initially predicted. While these last seven years have not been easy, I feel they have been the best years of my life. Even as I write this, it sounds crazy. Yet it is true. Maybe it is because I appreciate each day more.

Disruptions can cause us to become self-focused. We can start asking, "why me" and thinking about what could have been. In moments like those, we tend to lose hope and feel the weight of the world press down upon us. Rather than dwell there, might it be better to think about how to make the most of each day we have? How do you want to invest the remainder of your life?

## Some questions to help us make the most of each day:

- Who are the people you want to invest in? Family members, co-workers, community members, and church members.
- What are you currently doing that gives you life that lifts your spirit? How can you do more of that?
- Are there things (or people) that seem to rob you of hope and joy? Is there a way to spend less time in those areas?
- What have you learned along your journey? What have life's disruptions taught you? Would anyone benefit from what you have learned?
- Have you ever considered joining any community, church, or service groups? How could you help them?
- Is there someone you could write, text, email, or call who would be encouraged to know someone is thinking about them? Could you reach out to them once a week?
- What have you always wanted to do? What is on your bucket list? Take a moment to write it out. Are there things you can do? You might have to adjust some things due to the disruption, but I bet you can find some exciting things to do. Whom would you want to join you on the adventure?

- As you think about life, what is the balance of activity and quiet you find helpful right now? Have you shared that with others in your life?

**How would you complete the following statements:**

- I am concerned that when my life comes to an end, I will not have _____
- I will have peace and be content for the remainder of my life if I _____

# WHERE DOES MY
# STUFF GO?

My (Dan) mother was an only child. As her grandparents, aunts, uncles, and parents passed away, she ended up with most of the "family treasures." Her corner cabinet and a few other places became a "museum" of Entrikin family history. One afternoon when Nancy and I were visiting, we sent Joseph and Rayann off on an adventure with their grandfather. We sat with mom as she slowly picked up each piece of china, silverware, or nick-nack and slowly told its story. She spoke of where it came from, who owned it, and why it was important to her. As we listened, I tried to capture each story and record it for history. Mom had little patience for retelling a story once she had moved on to another piece. When we were done, I printed out our record, and mom smiled that we had captured a piece of the history that was so important to her. She had been concerned that people might forget the important stories behind the pieces. Her mind was at rest.

What is most important as you think about those things you have collected over the years? What history do you want to be passed down to future generations? Can a family member or friend help you capture those stories? While your gut reaction may be that nobody is interested, my sense is that you will be surprised by who wants to hear your stories.

Capturing the stories and history is much easier today. Most cell phones have excellent cameras and can record great video. Consider asking a family member (especially a child or grandchild) to help you capture some of what you want to pass along. Sharing your stories could be one of the greatest gifts you leave your loved ones.

## PRACTICAL STEPS

If you are like me (Dan), you have looked around your home and thought, when something happens to me, I hope (insert name) ends up with this. It is not that you are looking to leave anytime soon. This is just a natural way to think about the material items that are important to you.

In order for your wishes to become a reality, you must record them in some fashion and share the record. It is not enough to tell "Jimmy" you want him to have your favorite . A part of you might feel this is morbid or fatalistic thinking. In reality, it is wise planning to ensure that what is important to you ends up where you want it to.

One of the places this is real for me (Dan) is my library. Over the years I have amassed quite a collection of books. For a book to be "real," I need to feel the pages. This means I have way too many books in my study. Standing before my shelves, there are moments I will think, "I hope (insert name) ends up with this book." There are different reasons. Sometimes I know they would enjoy the book, and other times the author explains something that could be life-changing for my friend. Whatever the reason, there is little chance of it happening if I do not clearly communicate my thoughts.

Making your wishes known and communicating them clearly can relieve some added stress from your caregiver. It is not uncommon for people who have faded into the mist during one of life's disruptions to suddenly reappear when it is time to divide what has been left behind. It is not uncommon for those who have been least available to help care for a loved one to have some of the strongest feelings about what should be done with what has been left behind.

If you do not provide guidance, it can lead to conflict that only adds stress to a season filled with anxiety. So instead, look at this planning as helping your loved ones move through their grief and toward healing in the healthiest way possible.

## Act Now

For years I had a rather large wood shop. Our home is filled with furniture from my time spent in the shop. There were many Christmases where every gift we gave family and friends came out of my shop.

When we moved from North Carolina to Pennsylvania, I rented a separate truck to move the tools and supplies. My only requirement for our new home in Pennsylvania was a two-car garage to turn it into the sacred space of my wood shop.

One year after my diagnosis, the shop was in disarray, and I had no energy to finish setting it up. I did not have the energy to stand in the shop like before. Spending time with the machines was less joyful and even dangerous, as I grew tired quickly.

My focus shifted from the shop to writing and other projects. At first, I resisted the shift. Slowly I came to realize it was a good thing. Walking through a garage full of unused machines did not make sense. One afternoon I stood looking at all the equipment and realized that if something happened to me, Nancy would be left to deal with a bunch of equipment she knew very little about.

I made the decision that I would clean out my shop. My drill press went to a young man just starting his shop. Standing in my driveway, watching his wife help him load it into their truck, I was reminded of how I built my shop years ago. It felt good to watch my tools find a new home. I felt even better knowing Nancy would not have to deal with them. (Be sure to read the chapter, *Perspectives*, to see how I did not fully understand her feelings about this process. We should have talked before I started selling things.).

My point is that with the proper conversations with those closest to you, there are probably steps you can take now to ensure that some of your stuff finds a good home.

## SOME QUESTIONS TO HELP THE PROCESS OF DEALING WITH STUFF:

- Can you make a list of those things you consider valuable or memorable?
- Are there items you want to keep around you that provide good memories? For example, I got rid of my fly-tying station and all my fly fishing gear – except my fly rod, which hangs on my wall as a reminder of great times on the river.
- As you look at certain things, do you envision specific people enjoying them in the future? How have you communicated your desire for them to have these special items?
- Are there steps you could take right now that would help with the process of dealing with your stuff?
- Are there steps you can take to help your caregiver and/or family navigate the process of dealing with your things with grace and a sense of peace?
- How does your caregiver or family feel about your process for dealing with material things? Have you

talked about it? Keep in mind there are many different perspectives on the same disruption.

- Is there a group or organization that might benefit from some of the treasures you have accumulated? For example, if you have collected books, might you donate them to a library?

# WHEN TIME IS SHORT

Beyond the death of my grandparents, I had not experienced the death of a close family member when Dan was diagnosed. After Dan's diagnosis of what is most likely a terminal illness, I have not been able to imagine what the experience of losing him will be like. I ache for what he will go through. I ache for what I will feel. I ache for my children and others who care.

My personal goal has been to love Dan enough to be willing to let him go when that time comes. If his days on this earth are coming to an end, I want to put his needs first. I want to be willing to support him when treatments are no longer helpful and need to stop. When doctors say Dan's comfort needs to come first versus fighting the illness longer, I want Dan to be the priority. For seven years, I have struggled with a desire to hold onto Dan forever while preparing myself to let him go.

I don't know if I will pass that test or not. But I hope I am strong enough to give Dan precisely what he needs when that time comes. In May of 2021, Dan was in the hospital in Philadelphia. It seemed that his time was at an end. I was in the hospital hallway having a few ZOOM meetings with co-workers as Dan rested in his room. Some co-workers knew what was happening behind the scenes, and some did not. But talking to my boss, I said, "I apologize now for this conversation, but it looks like hospice is coming soon. Possibly at the end of this hospital stay. We need to talk about what work will look like for me during Dan's final days." After being caught off guard, Caroline rallied to my support, and we worked out a part-time work plan that I never had to implement. But I did have to start considering how to handle Dan's final days.

Again, it is hard to project what will happen, but I have assigned myself as the gatekeeper. When Dan is struggling with his final days, I will decide who talks to him and who does not. Dan will have the final say, but no one will get to Dan without going through me first. There are family members we have begged to talk to us for the last several years, but they have refused any contact because of "strained relations" with Dan. Those people will not have the chance to bare their souls with Dan during those final days. They have known he has a terminal illness for six years. There has been time to mend relationships. That chance will end when the last days are near. [Dan here – as Nancy and I have discussed this, I am glad she will serve in this role. In fact, I have had a few conversations with others who can support her during what will be a difficult season]

On the opposite side, I hope we can share final moments and words with the dear friends and family members who have been such a support over the years. I hope we can have time to celebrate a well-lived life while Dan is with us.

When Dan turned fifty, we were thrilled he made this milestone age. But unfortunately, cancer was not going well, and Dan did not have a lot of energy for large groups of people. So I handed him a "party in a box" on his birthday. I collected letters from many people we have known through the years. Our friends and family sent photos, memories, and thoughts. I hope we can share memories and smiles during a time that may also be difficult and sad.

## QUESTIONS TO CONSIDER FOR THE FINAL DAYS:

- Who will make the final decision to end treatments?
- Where does the patient want to spend the final days? At home or in a care facility? Is this possible? Has the patient discussed this with the caregiver (s)?
- Who will decide who spends time with the patient during those final days?
- How will friends hear about the progression of the illness?

# HOSPICE

## WITH JOAN HOLLIDAY

Hospice care focuses on the total care of terminally ill patients. Many doctors and hospitals focus primarily on the medical care of patients, but hospice care gives equal attention to physical, psychological, and spiritual care for dying patients. Hospice services have been a tremendous help to the person facing death, the entire family, and all caregivers. In many ways, Hospice is another support system to help individuals and their families as they travel this difficult journey.

As a pastor, I am intimately familiar with hospice. I have helped families connect with Hospice services for care and support. I cannot think of a single negative interaction with a hospice nurse or provider. They are the ultimate caregivers who come alongside patients and families during the most challenging times of their lives.

When many people hear of hospice, they immediately think about imminent end-of-life issues. What comes to mind is care provided in the final hours of life to help bring peace and comfort during the transition from this life to the next.

That is one piece of Hospice's work. But, in reality, Hospice is much more. Hospice is:

*Medical care for people with an anticipated life expectancy of 6 months or less, when cure isn't an option, and the focus shifts to symptom management and quality of life.* [1]

You will find the hospice website (hospicefoundation.org) very helpful. The website provides helpful guidance on when it would be appropriate to consider requesting hospice services. This decision is something your doctor can assist you with.

Hospice should be considered when:

*There is a significant decline in physical and/or cognitive status despite medical treatment. This may include increased pain or other symptoms, substantial weight loss, extreme fatigue, shortness of breath, or weakness.*

*The goal is to live more comfortably and forego the often physically debilitating treatments that have been unsuccessful in curing or halting a life-threatening illness.*

*Life expectancy is 6 months or less, according to physicians.*

*The person is in the end stage of Alzheimer's or dementia.* [2]

Nancy and I invited our good friend Joan Holliday to help assemble some of the hospice-related questions. Joan has been a community nurse for many years and has supported individuals and families facing terminal illnesses.

## AS YOU CONSIDER HOSPICE:

- Do you know someone who has used Hospice services?
- To many, the word Hospice is synonymous with "giving up." Is this true for you?
- How do you think about Hospice?
- How do your loved ones think about Hospice?
- Have you discussed Hospice with your physician?
- Did you know that the physician needs to make the referral to Hospice?
- Did you know that only a physician can state that the dying person has less than six months to live to be eligible for Hospice? Did you know someone can also be re-enrolled, and no one knows when the end of life will occur?
- Did you know that Medicare and Medicaid cover the expense of Hospice?
- Did you know that you can stop Hospice if your health improves or your illness goes into remission? Did you know you can stop Hospice at any time?

## PROCESS OF DYING:

As difficult as the discussion may be, the following questions will support the process of dying with dignity.

- Do you want to die at home?
- Do you know what room could accommodate you for dying at home?
- Do you have help to make any necessary changes to your home, so a stay at home is possible?

- Do you have the financial resources to pay for help in the home?
- Do you want to make the decision about what medications you take?
- Do you want to make the decision about what tests you will have?
- Do you want medications to provide you comfort as you are dying?
- Do you want to set up sessions with a counselor or a pastor?
- Do you and your family members need a compassionate person to talk to outside the family that understands the dying process?
- Do you want someone on-call for support 24 hours/day, seven days a week when the status of your loved one changes?

## QUESTIONS TO ASK HOSPICE PROVIDERS:

- Is the hospice provider certified and licensed by the state or federal government?
- Does the hospice provider train caregivers to care for you at home?
- How will your doctor work with the doctor from the hospice provider?
- Will the hospice staff meet regularly with you and your family to discuss care?
- How does the hospice staff respond to after-hour emergencies?
- What measures are in place to ensure hospice care quality?

- What services do hospice volunteers offer? Are they trained?
- Does the hospice provider have an inpatient facility to move someone to if needed?

# CARING THROUGH ISOLATION

*This journey of serious illness has been tumultuous. Full of ups and downs.*
But we have done it together each step of the way.
United, you have allowed me to walk alongside you.
I have been able to uphold, support, and share with you.

*Isolation adds a new dimension to this path. Apart, it seems somehow harder.*
News is not as easy to obtain or understand.
Worry creeps in when I cannot see you or talk to you.
Imagination takes the place of fact and knowledge.

*Reasons for separation vary, and the length of distance may change.*
Sometimes treatment requires the patient to stay apart.
Family responsibilities may prohibit visits to a loved one.
For us, rules and fears of germs were the cause.

*My fear was that after all this time, you were navigating seriousness
alone.*
Anxiety would overcome me each day as I waited to hear.
Pressure was placed on you to obtain, process, and pass on
The information that was given then revoked and then changed.

*Watching a loved one suffer is heart-wrenching and sad. Nothing one
desires.*
But to see it from afar brings tears and despair.
Being together again brought relief and gladness.
And hope that we will not have to be apart again.[1]

©Nancy Nicewonger 2020 *Nancy wrote this reflection when Dan was
in the hospital during the start of COVID. Nancy was not allowed into
the hospital. This was the first time we traveled our journey separated
from each other.*

# Part Six
# When You Think About Me

Grief is one of the most powerful emotions we will ever experience. It can make us feel as if the entire world is standing still and there is no hope for the future.

Everyone who loves will one-day experience loss and grief. Unfortunately, our culture is so focused on avoiding pain that we do very little to help people navigate seasons of grief well. While the world appears focused on moving forward, those grieving often feel left alone to deal with their pain and loss.

In the following chapters, we speak to the process of mourning and grief. Healing begins as we go through this most difficult of seasons. We are joined by three friends who help us think about walking with others who are grieving, becoming a healthy grievers, and preparing a memorial service. A memorial service is often the first step toward healing.

# Grief Is Hard – But Necessary

## with Pastor Annalie Korengel

As we start to write, I want to be clear, neither Nancy nor myself are grief experts. What I mean by that is that we have not attended any classes, seminars, or training that dealt with grief. Instead, like many others, we have traveled the difficult road of mourning and loss. As we share, we speak from our experience.

While there may be familiar stages of grief, everyone mourns in their own way. To expect everyone's grieving to look or sound the same is unrealistic and damaging. To help us understand this idea, think about an imaginary family with three children. One child is quiet and reflective, the other constantly seeking attention, while the third is all about taking care of what needs to be done. Expecting all three children to grieve similarly would be ridiculous. The quiet and reflective child would need time away from everyone to process their emotions. Child two might find solace sitting in a room full of people telling stories about the one they have lost. The third child could find comfort in making sure that all the details surrounding a family gathering celebrating the one lost were in order.

I have watched relationships damaged as someone insists that everyone grieve as they do. Grief is hard. We need to allow people the space to mourn in a way that is meaningful to them.

Personally, I (Dan) fall more into the quiet, reflective, taking care of what needs to be done side of grieving. Giving space to those who grieve in more expressive ways is not always easy. A part of me wants to tell them to "do that in private" or "if they get about doing something, they will feel better." Neither of those thoughts are helpful. Allowing people the space to grieve in the way most helpful for **them** is a gift.

I (Dan) have walked alongside people struggling with grief. They did not feel they were "doing it right." Maybe the tears were not flowing, or there was anger mixed in with the sense of loss. For some, they simply did not feel anything. At the moment, they were numb. Extend yourself grace. Grief is a funny thing. It is hard to predict, and we can be overwhelmed at what feels like unusual times. There is no "right way" to grieve.

We slowly lost my mom over decades. Dementia is cruel. I mourned the loss of my mother while she was still physically with us. Her funeral felt like something we had been marching toward for years. As mom was laid to rest, I was focused on helping my dad get through the day. Then, two months after my mother passed away, I cleaned out her wallet. Sitting in my study, fresh waves of grief swept over me. Holding her wallet, I could picture mom frantically searching through the different compartments for her driver's license or some special card. She used to get so worked up and never allowed anyone to help her find what was "lost." I would get frustrated. Sitting in my study, that memory brought a smile to my face. I miss mom. Grief is a funny thing.

If you are walking alongside someone with a long-term illness, there are two additional pieces to the grief journey. First, you have been grieving since the day of diagnosis. In small and large ways, you have been processing the loss of your loved one since the day you heard a doctor tell you of the disease. Looking back, you will have gone through the stages of grief. There will have been times of letting go and a renewed commitment to fight. This will be especially true if there have been moments when it felt like you would lose your loved one, only to have them make a miraculous recovery. When your loved one passes away, there may be a very real sense in which you will have already completed your grieving process. The longer the journey, the more real this could be. People around you may be "surprised" by the loss of your loved one. For them, the loss will only become real when your loved one passes away. As they process their grief, they may look at your "strength" and comment on how you are handling the loss. Some may encourage you to grieve in a way that fits their idea of what grief looks like. Extend yourself grace, you have been grieving since the day of diagnosis, and everyone grieves in their own way.

Second, there may be another feeling that is harder to deal with than grief or loss. I (Dan) have walked with many caregivers who have wrestled with a sense of relief when their loved ones passed away. Caregiving is an overwhelming job. The longer one is a caregiver, the harder it can be. When life is focused on patient care, it is easy for entire days to be spent dealing with issues like doctor appointments, health insurance, providing medications at the correct times, feeding, and bathing. Emotionally everyone is on edge. The caregiver moves through each day in fear of the day when the worst thing possible will happen.

When that day finally arrives, it is almost a sense of relief. Their loved one is no longer in pain, the stress of caregiving is gone, and they no longer live in fear of what might happen. In a strange sort of way, the caregiver is set free to focus on their life. There is a joy associated with that reality. Immediately that joy is met with guilt. The only reason their life is like this is because their loved one is gone. What a terrible person they must be. In a very real way, the sense of freedom and joy caregivers often feel as they move forward in life is harder to deal with than the sense of grief or loss. One of the reasons it is more difficult to process is that people are often surprised by it. Do not be surprised. Extend yourself grace.

We asked our friend, Pastor Annalie Korengel, to share her experience about what it means to walk well alongside those who are grieving.

In my over twenty years as a grief counselor, hospice chaplain, and church minister, I have had the privilege of officiating many funerals and walking alongside grieving people. The one thing I always say is, "Grief is hard – but necessary. It will come out one way or another." I hope this section helps you find the many resources available for those who are grieving.

Grief is the natural cost of loving someone. Grief is not selfish, nor is it a sign of faithlessness. It is an appropriate expression of love. It is also hard, even exhausting, work that does not move in a linear fashion. The five stages (by Elizabeth Kubler-Ross) often referenced in death, dying, and grief were never intended to be linear or a one-size-fits-all checklist. There is also no "endpoint."

Grief typically follows a wave-like pattern, which may ease over time, but never completely goes away. The death of a loved one is not something you "get over." Instead, you learn to cope, adjust, and manage the changes in your life.

Those who grieve are often told that the first year is the hardest, but that is most often not the case. The early weeks and months after a death are often filled with activities (funerals, wills, going through items, filing forms, waiting for paperwork) that make life seem like a blur. As a result, grief often gets put on the back burner.

Give yourself permission to grieve. Create space to acknowledge the different emotions that come with a loss. Try to stick to a daily routine whenever possible. Eat regularly and make sure you stay hydrated (this seems trivial, but grief is dehydrating, and being dehydrated makes everything seem worse!) Focus on self-care. Seek medical advice and care if you think you might be ill or depressed.

Reach out for support. Staying connected with family and friends is especially important when you are grieving. Take advantage of the many resources available to you. (see list below)

Many people will say, "Let me know if you need anything;" some of them really mean it. Take advantage of that. Have a list ready of things they can do to help: pet care, child care or transportation, meals, yard work, errands, laundry, etc. Do not be shy about sharing your needs with those who offer to help. When someone says, "Let me know if you need anything," be quick to share what you need. The truth is they feel at a loss for how to help. Your speaking about a specific need helps them feel helpful and a part of the healing process.

The grief of children is different from that of an adult. It is influenced by many things, especially age and family dynamics. It is important to remember that each child's or teen's experience is unique to them, even in the same family. Younger children often work through grief while playing, and teens often turn to their peers for support.

Encourage kids to ask questions. Answer the question that they ask honestly (do not give more information than they ask for). Encourage their curiosity about the person who died. Always tell them the truth; it comes out eventually, and they should always hear it from a trusted adult.

Let them know that their range of thoughts and emotions are accepted. Have mutual respect for their opinions and choices – and provide choices whenever you can. Keep discipline and schedules consistent. Spend time talking and remembering, but always on their terms. Find ways for kids to stay connected to the person who has died.

If you are invited into the sacred space of walking with someone in their grief journey, there are ways you can help. The most important thing is to be a good listener! They may not be asking for advice or solutions; they just want to be heard. Respect their way of grieving and accept mood swings. Help out with practical tasks. Someone grieving may be unable to tell you what they need, so make specific suggestions: pet care, childcare or transportation, laundry, meals, etc., and make sure you follow through with the task. Stay connected and available. One thing to avoid is to try to explain the loss or make unhelpful platitudes ("they are in a better place," "God needed an angel," etc.) Instead, be sincere and offer words that touch the heart.

The most important thing you can do for anyone grieving is to say the name of the deceased and tell their stories. The great poet and philosopher Cicero wrote, "The life of the dead is set in the memories of the living."

## RESOURCES FOR THOSE WHO ARE GRIEVING:

- For military and law enforcement families, check out TAPS.org.
- Check out your local hospice agency or hospital for bereavement groups (usually available to anyone, regardless of where the death occurred).
- Talk to your pastor, rabbi, imam, or other spiritual leader.
- Book/journal combination: "Understanding Your Grief" by Alan D. Wolfelt, Ph.D.
- Ask your funeral director for recommendations.
- Many yoga studios offer special classes for those experiencing grief.
- Ask your physician for a recommendation for a mental health provider if that is needed.

- Seek out a trained grief counselor.

## Resources for grieving children:

- "A Little Blue Bottle," by Jennifer Grant.
- "The Next Place," by Warren Hanson.
- "Giants," by A. E. McIntyre.
- "A Parent's Guide to Grieving Children," by Phyllis R. Silverman and Madelyn Kelly.
- Many hospitals have bereavement groups for children and teens.
- Camp Erin: https://elunanetwork.org/camps-programs/camp-erin.

# Learning To Be A Healthy Griever

## with Chaplain Tony Tilford

We asked our friend, Chaplain Tony Tilford, to share his thoughts about healthy grieving. Tony has worked hard to deal well with the loss that has been a part of his life. He shares lessons learned in the darkest of times in the hopes of helping others deal better with seasons of grief. Listen as Chaplain Tony helps us think about what it means to be a *healthy griever*.

It has been said that "to live is to grieve," and anyone who has lived long enough to reflect on their life will most likely agree. Especially when understanding grief as being both more and larger than just the loss of someone to death—though the loss of a spouse/partner, child, and other relations clearly exacts the greatest toll.

So, the question at hand is not "do we, or will we grieve?" Grief cannot be helped, but the more important question might be: "Do we grieve in a healthy way?" Sociologists have long agreed that most modern cultures (and family units) do not prepare their members to grieve in appropriate and healthy ways. But what does it mean to be a healthy griever? Here are some suggestions.

Since many find it easy to learn and recall things presented in easily recognizable formats, we present an acronym to help you understand what healthy grieving looks like. That acronym is G.R.I.E.V.E. Yes, that's right, the word grieve itself is used to set down some tasks that many consider essential aspects of the healthy grieving process. One last point to keep in mind before we give those tasks to you; they are not stages or phases. They do not proceed from one to another in order of their appearance.

Here we go.

**Give time to yourself.** Do not be pressured by anyone, or yourself, to feel that you "should be over this by now." Everyone grieves in their own way, unique to their situation and personality. It is good to work on one's grief at one's own pace. Keep this as a motto for your grieving—"Give it time, but give time to it."

**Receive from others.** Be careful not to be too self-reliant and independent. In your loss/grief, many people will offer help in ways they feel might make things better for you—offer meals, their presence, and other support. Be open to letting others in.

**Invite others to journey with you.** Beyond receiving what is offered, you may want to step out and ask for help. This may include getting some counsel from sympathetic friends or even professionals in the grieving field.

**Examine your life.** In particular, look to your past experiences of grief and loss, and ask yourself whether you were able to mourn them adequately. When we haven't grieved properly, the grief experts say that we carry that grief with us, in our bodies, in our emotions, and it cries out for the attention we did not give it before. This helps explain why many are so easily triggered to tears and sadness while saying, "I do not know where that came from."

**Value yourself.** This is so important. Be careful of thoughts of inappropriate shame or worthlessness; these can hinder your healing. There is a love of/for oneself that is healthy and opens the door often to being loved by others.

**Expect that there will be good and bad days ahead.** There will be times when some trigger (a smell, song, picture, etc.) will cause an emotional response, bringing you down, often quite unexpectedly and quickly. Because grieving is a life-long journey, you need to be very patient with yourself.

As you deal with your loss, keep in mind the tasks above. Again, they are not meant to be stages you go through. However, it might be a good idea to take time to see if you have perhaps already been practicing them in your life, especially if your loss was a recent one.

## QUESTIONS RELATING TO HEALTHY GRIEVING TASKS:

- Have I been patient with myself and recognized I need time to heal?
- Have I been aware that I need to give some time to my healing?
- Have I been open to receiving from others? Who? Why not?
- Who have I invited to travel alongside me in my grief journey? Who might I ask?
- Am I willing to take the time to examine my past grief experiences?
- Do I value myself? In what ways do I do that? Or not do that?

- Have I experienced any triggered emotional responses? For example, are there moments when someone or something causes waves of grief to wash over me? Do I find myself reacting emotionally in settings that did not previously evoke such emotion? Why?

# HELPING LOVED ONES GRIEVE

## WITH MATT GRIECO

Thinking about funeral arrangements is a reality for those facing a terminal illness. Each person will approach this topic in their own way. Some will want to talk about it in great detail, while others will not want to speak about it. Neither one is right or wrong. However, it is essential to recognize that while one person may not want to talk about funeral arrangements, others may find it necessary. As with everything else, the challenge will be to navigate this subject carefully to address the needs of everyone involved.

Personally, this was something I (Dan) had to talk about. There was something about my funeral that paralyzed me. I was obsessed with how it would be handled. A part of me felt frozen until I sat down and planned my memorial service, met with the funeral director, and arranged for all the participants in the service. Once that work was done, I could get about living life to the fullest. Nancy will tell you I was looking to have control over something one last time in my life. She may be right; our world was pretty out of control at the time.

Before we talk about some things you might consider in making funeral arrangements, I want to share some wisdom that a friend shared with me. Matt Grieco is a funeral director; he will be taking care of my service. As we sat down and reviewed everything I had prepared, he reminded me,

*"Dan, it is good for Nancy to have some decisions to make as part of the grieving process. There is something healing and helpful about having something to do while she is grieving losing you."*

If you are a planner like me, resist the temptation to plan everything. Instead, leave a few decisions to be made by others. It will help them mourn your loss and begin the healing process.

With that said, there are plenty of things that can be thought about prior to death. Answering some of these questions might be one of the greatest gifts you can leave your loved ones. Therefore, it might be wise to create a notebook or file containing answers to questions like these so they can be found easily when the time comes.

I invited Matt to help compile some of the questions related to funeral plans. Some of his thoughts deal specifically with making funeral arrangements. Others come from decades of walking alongside families during life's most challenging times.

## QUESTIONS TO HELP EVERYONE APPROACH THE REALITY OF DEATH IN A HEALTHY WAY:

- Are your survivors in denial or dealing with your eventual departure? Do they know how to grieve, why to grieve, and how to heal?
- Have they ever experienced a significant loss, like what will be felt when you are gone?
- What are your thoughts about death and dying?

- Have you had "The talk of a lifetime" so your family knows your history, where you came from, what's most important to you, what you're proud of, and what you plan/planned to do?
- Does your spouse or partner have an advocate or "death Duala" or anyone to assist them with transition tasks? There will be things to do before and after the passing.
- Have you considered your legacy? What are the character traits, teachings, and lessons you hope your family received from you?
- Have you considered video-recorded messages to each person you love to be viewed after you have gone?
- What is your long-range plan as a survivor? It is important to remember that when you hit deep grief, accomplishing tasks will be difficult and should be delayed anyway to allow your body time to heal.

## THE MEMORIAL SERVICE

- Is there a specific funeral home you would like to care for your service?
- Do you have insurance or pre-paid funeral arrangements? If so, where can the policy be found?
- Do you have any convictions regarding burial or cremation?
- Who will lead the ceremony? A memorial service is often the first step in the grieving/healing process.
- Do you have favorite songs or scriptures you want to be included in any services?
- Are there any people you would like to speak at your service?

- Are you sure no one will hijack the funeral with insensitive words or ideas? Every word said will resonate forever, good or bad. Who can help make sure that does not happen?
- Have you written your obituary, or will loved ones do this for you?
- Do you want memorial contributions to go to a specific charity or cause?

# LOVING THROUGH LONG-TERM ILLNESS

I have loved my man for over twenty-seven years, starting with my second decade of life. Now nearing the end of my forties, we have been faced with a long-term illness. A few months ago, I would have called it a terminal illness, but there is currently hope that this may not be the end. Our loving will continue.

During this time, we have felt a closeness even though there was an overriding sadness at times. I took a few moments around month 8 of our journey to consider some of the blessings and challenges I have experienced. Not being the one going through the sickness, I often feel self-centered, dwelling on my feelings. However, I have learned that dealing with my emotions keeps me stronger when he needs help with his.

Here is my list of how I experience life as a caregiver from our first year dealing with cancer.

## BLESSINGS:

- Each day together now feels like a gift.

- I treasure the experiences we have and store them as memories.
- We rely upon and value one another more than we did previously. (In my opinion).
- We can talk to one another and plan for our futures.
- I have been able to talk to a financial advisor about life on my own and have a plan for our house and expenses.
- Dan has taught me how to change the water filters, and I practiced snow removal.
- I have decided if you throw the mouse trap out along with the mouse, you don't have to touch anything.
- I have started forging relationships with others that will aid me in times of despair.
- We have learned how to share responsibilities at work to allow him to continue his job as long as possible.
- I have renewed a relationship with my brother in a new and life-giving way.
- OK is my new standard. An OK day can be good enough.
- I have learned how to relieve stress on my own. Pulling weeds is often my chosen weapon.
- I now understand caregiving. I now know I didn't understand before.
- Knowing I can hold his hand, be his help and love him always. A true blessing.

## CHALLENGES:

- I am tired. A lot.
- I lay awake at night listening to him breathe because I feel safe when he is breathing.
- Medical bills are necessary but stress-giving.

- Anger comes when I get pulled away from helping him to fulfill another task.
- Balancing home, work, children, friends, and self.
- Finding time to use the gift certificate for the spa day.
- Being content with our life.
- Seeing an elderly couple brings resentment that we may not get those golden years together.
- I am tired—a lot.
- Wanting to say, "How do you feel?" too often.
- Having a lack of patience when he is ill-tempered and short with me.
- Resenting people who say, "I know he'll be fine."
- Resenting that the doctor won't say, "He'll be fine."
- Spending hours on the phone about referrals and insurance and lab mistakes.
- Dealing with a sadness that has had a place in my heart since the day of diagnosis.
- I am not coming to the aid of others because I am too focused on myself.
- Fear that I won't be strong enough to let him go when the end comes.
- Wishing it could have been me instead of him.
- Knowing all I can do is hold his hand, be his help, and love him always.

How does one reconcile those blessings and challenges?

Life goes on. It doesn't give you time to reason out your feelings. When the challenges are overcome, the blessings, love, and faith give me hope. When each step becomes heavy, I start looking for a blessing, for I cling to them.

Where do I see God?

The fact that I feel blessed during this journey comes from

having peace with God. Amidst the challenges, I can question and fall apart before God and know I am still loved.

While I don't know that God ordained this path, I know He still offers life to the full. It may not be the life I planned, but It will be the one God journeys beside me on. When I rest in God, I notice the blessings more often.

To God be praise, even when my heart bleeds tears. [1]

© Nancy Nicewonger 2017

# PART SEVEN
# SPIRITUAL JOURNEY

Many in our culture treat the spiritual life as a luxury. We will get around to tending to it once all the other areas of our lives are in relative peace. Let me focus on my job; I can tend to my spiritual life once I am settled. My family life is crazy right now; let me focus there, once the family is settled, I will explore the spiritual. I am so tired; what I need is a series of vacations. When I return from this trip, I will feel refreshed and focus on the spiritual.

As we all know, rarely does life settle down. It can best be described as a roller coaster ride. Ups and downs, twists and turns, things finally settle down only as the ride is about to end.

Investing in our spiritual life is one of the smartest things we can do as we seek to navigate this world with grace, peace, and hope.

# A Journey Like No Other

My spiritual journey did not begin the day I received my diagnosis. I have been a seeker most of my life.

The teachings and life of Jesus have challenged me to live a life of grace, love, and peace. I am drawn to the stories where Jesus extends grace and focuses on the needs of those struggling with life.

I draw hope and encouragement as Jesus demonstrates what it means to truly see the fullness of a person and remain in relationship with them. His example reminds me of the words of the writer in Psalm 42.

*"Deep calls to Deep"*

— Psalm 42:7 (NIV)

I have come to understand those words to mean the depth, the fullness of who I am calling out to God, the fullness of God calling out to me. Deep calls to Deep. One of the most significant challenges on any spiritual journey is learning to discern the Spirit's calling to us. The depth of God, calling out to the fullness, the completeness, of who we are.

Watching Jesus interact with his world, I see the fullness of God calling out to all of humanity. As Jesus launches his public ministry, he quotes from the scroll of Isaiah,

> *"The Spirit of the Lord is on me,*
>   *because he has anointed me*
>   *to proclaim good news to the poor.*
> *He has sent me to proclaim freedom for the*
>     *prisoners*
>   *and recovery of sight for the blind,*
> *to set the oppressed free,*
> *to proclaim the year of the Lord's favor."*

— LUKE 4:17-19 (NIV)

Other translations use language such as "set captives free" or "free those who are oppressed." Unfortunately, there is much within our world that holds people captive, much that oppresses the human spirit. Freedom is a good thing. Freedom to experience the best God has for us.

In a bizarre way, cancer has set me free.

As I write this, I am nearing my eighth year of living with cancer. My oncologist says we will never use words like "cured" or "remission" when discussing my cancer. I am three cycles into my sixth round of systemic chemotherapy as this book is going to print.

It may seem contradictory to say, "cancer set me free" while it still ravages my body. Yet that is my truth. I believe two seemingly opposite ideas can be true at the same time. My time in the scriptures has taught me to see the world this way.

Scripture refers to King David as a "man after God's own heart" (1 Samuel 13:14, Acts 13:22). Yet, he was an adulterer and murderer (2 Samuel 11-12). Two very opposite ideas true at the same time.

The Apostle Paul was both a persecutor of Christians and one of the greatest missionaries the church has ever seen.

Peter, Jesus' disciple, had enough courage to get out of a boat during a raging storm to walk on water with Jesus (Matthew 14:22-33). However, this same Peter denied Jesus three times in the days leading up to Jesus' crucifixion (Luke 22:54-62).

Christians speak of Jesus being crucified, dead, buried, AND resurrected!

My faith has taught me that two seemingly opposite or conflicting ideas can be true simultaneously.

My cancer is killing me, AND it has set me free. There are moments when I tend to focus on one truth more than the other. In darker seasons, I dwell on the challenges and the reality that no matter how well each treatment works, my cancer always grows back. On brighter days, I tend to focus on how cancer has set me free to grow into who I am today. My best days come when I can balance the reality that cancer is trying to kill me with the truth that the Spirit is using the struggle to help me experience "life to the full."

How does the Spirit use my cancer to set me free?

**Cancer helped me face my mortality.** There is something about hearing someone in a white coat say, "Get your affairs in order," which causes you to think. I thought I understood my mortality, but I did not. There were seasons of wrestling with life, healing, and what comes afterward.

I finally landed in this place where I will live each day as if I am healed, as if my cancer is no more. The truth is I believe God could remove my cancer from me if that were the Spirit's will. I also believe that God could work through the amazing doctors who care for me to bring about my healing. Ultimately, I believe that when I pass away, I will experience total healing. My healing is

NOT a question of IF; it remains a question of WHEN and WHERE.

Cancer helped me face my mortality and allowed me to live each day as if I am already healed!

**Cancer helped me focus on that which is most important.** Cancer granted me clarity. Tell someone that time is short, and suddenly, they can focus on what is important. With limited energy and time, I got clear on what was important and valuable to me. I also got clear on what I did not want to "waste time" on. That clarity helped me set aside many things that were filling my time. For example, I got clear that I would rather spend an afternoon talking with people than preparing for a meeting. Investing in people seemed a better use of my limited energy. Nancy had always been a priority. How I expressed that became much more precise. I looked at some of what was filling my calendar and found ways to "let it go" as I made time for those people and things which mattered most.

Moving in such a way meant I was living my best life. I was investing myself in the right places and spending time where I could make a difference. Cancer helped set me free.

**Cancer caused me to slow down.** So much of my life has been spent rushing to achieve and obtain. Accomplish this so we can move forward with the next thing. Build, grow, complete, and compete so that people can see you have value. It is a trap many of us fall into.

While I had always been drawn to meditation and quiet, cancer and chemotherapy had a way of making me slow down. The brain fog of chemotherapy meant I could not think, plan, and strategize like before. Instead, I learned to be content to sit in the stillness and relax.

Slowing down allowed me to listen to myself. It allowed me to hear the struggle and emotions welling up from inside. I was in touch with my spirit in ways that eluded me for decades. Times of quiet were an invitation for the Spirit to speak. I began to see how the Spirit was present in the midst of the everyday and ordinary.

**Cancer has made me a nicer, gentler, kinder person.** I had an experience early on in my cancer journey which has shaped how I view the world. A few weeks into my journey, I was still processing my new normal. Grief, anger, fear, sadness, mourning, and a profound sense of loss were my constant companions.

I was at one of the weakest points of my journey. Physically, it felt like a gentle breeze, or a rushing toddler could knock me over. Emotionally I was all over the place.

Being that picture of health, I decided to go to one of the big box stores and search for noise-canceling headphones to help me navigate noisy chemo treatment rooms.

Entering the store, I looked (on the outside) like everything was okay. But, inside, I was a mess. The store was packed. I slowly made my way to the headphones. People jostled and bumped into me as I walked down the aisle. I finally stopped and grabbed a display counter for support to keep from falling over.

Standing there watching people rush by, my anger flared. Can't these people see **ME?!** Don't they know what **I AM** going through? Why are people so insensitive? I was near tears.

It was then that the Spirit spoke. Spoke gently but firmly. The Spirit helped me see myself and the world a little differently. It was transformative.

I realized that I looked like a pillar of strength from the outside. At 6' 5" and carrying a little more BMI than my doctor recommends, few people worry about knocking me over. Nobody in the store could see the cancer ravaging my body. Everyone was blind to the emotional mess that was my reality.

A second thought hit me as I watched the crowd move through the store. I wonder what struggles these people are going through. What realities of their lives remain hidden from me?

As people walked by, I started to see them differently. I stopped focusing on my struggles and began caring for the unseen hardships of those before me. Who else was fighting an illness? How many had recently lost a loved one? Which families were struggling to make ends meet? Where was divorce or relationship drama impacting someone's day?

I was overwhelmed by the reality that those swarming around me were most likely experiencing pain on a level I was unfamiliar with. Once again, I was near tears. But, this time, I was thinking about the pain found everywhere in our world. Leaving the store, I was the healthiest I had been in weeks.

Cancer has made me more aware of the pain within our world. It has made me more sensitive to the difficulties people experience each and every day. As a result, I am slower to judge and find it easier to extend grace and compassion. I tend to laugh more and take myself less seriously. I am looking to find joy in each moment. The moments have become increasingly special to me.

## DISCERNING THE SPIRIT'S INVITATION

In my thirties, I (Dan) was blessed to spend time with a spiritual director who helped me learn to be still and discern the Spirit's invitation for my life. Kit was a special guy who challenged me to see the world through a different lens. Kit, and his wife Tricia, played an important role in helping shape the way I see the world and encounter God. I am forever in their debt. While we have stayed in touch through the years, time has brought a distance between us. Twenty years later, I received Kit and Tricia's annual Christmas letter.

Listen as Tricia talks of walking as Kit's caregiver. Hear how she speaks of encountering God in the midst of tremendous struggle and heartache.

*We got a diagnosis in December 2019 of memory loss and possible dementia or Alzheimer's for Kit.*

*It has been a time of watching and experiencing Jesus' faithfulness through some major life challenges.*

*One of those challenges was getting COVID in 2020 and Kit ending up in the hospital. Then there was a mass found in my thyroid that was removed and, praise God, not cancerous. Kit also had shoulder surgery which caused post-surgical delirium, and then received a definite Alzheimer's diagnosis after a pet scan.*

*There is such a range of emotion and spiritual encounters in prayer with Jesus and life, that it can't all be detailed here. What I do know is, it's living in the difficulty of my own humanity and the humanity of those I love that pushes me to put total dependency of my life in the Lord's loving hands. I would not have it any other way. He is truly my sanctuary in the middle of the storm. He calls us to look at him, not at the storm. As I am aware of the storm around me, I rely on the love Jesus has for me, and His beauty around me to continue to do His ministry at Imagine, be Kit's caretaker, and feed into my children's lives.*

*Kit is still who he is in many ways. He is as good a drummer as he was years ago! He is having a harder time remembering conversations, writing, articulating words, and remembering details of our life and ministry, but he is very much at peace with God. He is still picking up books to read and shares something at that moment that surprises him or points him to God, but in a minute or two, it becomes a fleeting thought. This has been hard to watch. But, the Lord showed me to see it as it is, only in that moment. See Kit as He is, not as what Kit used to be. Grieving can swallow you up if you don't let Jesus direct you, connect with you in the weeping and carry it for you as you journey through it.*

*We are grateful for how God has used friends to help carry the load, by dropping by now and then to be with Kit and me.*

*We are excited to see what the Lord has for us to bring and to receive in the next year.* [1]

## Every journey has a beginning.

At the start of this chapter, I shared that my spiritual journey has been ongoing for years. There have been many twists, turns, and seasons. Cancer is just another stage or step along the path.

I have spent decades talking with people about their spiritual journeys. No two journeys have been the same. Each journey is as unique as the individual. No matter where you currently find yourself, seeker, doubter, agnostic, atheist, questioner, or someone overwhelmed with what life has brought your way, remember life is a journey. Seasons, no matter how difficult they may feel, will pass. New pieces of your journey will provide opportunities for growth. Do not allow what has been to determine what will be. Remain open to the depth of the Spirit calling out to the fullness of who you are.

Your story is just that...your story. I believe that no matter where you have been or what road you have traveled, the fullness of God's Spirit has been calling out to you along the way. I am going to close this chapter with a series of questions. They are designed to get you thinking about your journey and how to discern the Spirit's voice calling out to you. May you find a place of quiet and peace where the Spirit of the One who came "to set captives free" may speak to the depth of your soul.

SOME QUESTIONS TO HELP YOU REFLECT UPON YOUR SPIRITUAL JOURNEY:

## WHERE DO YOU SEE THE SPIRIT OF GOD AT WORK IN YOUR LIFE, IN YOUR WORLD?

- Who has come alongside to help you?
- When have you felt moments of peace during chaos?
- Did you ever find words to express a deeper emotion you did not know existed?
- Has someone (or a group of people) come alongside you to pray with you or support you spiritually?

## HAVE YOU FOUND A READING, SONG, OR SCRIPTURE THAT BROUGHT YOU PEACE?

- What is it about this particular thing that brings you peace?
- Have you experienced something like it before?

## IS THERE A LOCATION OR SPACE WHERE YOU FIND COMFORT?

- Why do you think this space brings you peace?
- Has this been true at other times in your life?

# ARE THERE PEOPLE YOU THINK OF AS SPIRITUAL GUIDES OR ROLE MODELS?

- How have these people helped shape the way you think about spiritual things? What about them would you most like to be true in your life?
- Is there someone you have walked alongside, read about, or encountered who challenges you spiritually? What draws your spirit to them?

# In Closing

## Emotions and Reactions

As you come to the end of this book, I (Dan) can imagine a wide range of emotions or reactions.

Maybe you are like Nancy. Thinking about the ideas or realities found within these pages often leaves her with a headache. A real, extreme, actual headache. For some, you will have a sense of relief, realizing you have already addressed many of the questions that were raised. Others will feel empowered. Having clear steps forward can often spur us on and lift our spirits.

We are confident that others will feel exhausted. Reading this book felt like a continual reminder of what was NOT done. You probably read in short chunks, laying the book aside as you did something else which spoke value into your life. For those who experienced the book this way, take heart; this is where Nancy and I began. To be honest, there are still moments when we feel this way. Times when the weight of the journey becomes too much, and it feels as if we are barely treading water. As life presses in, we must remember one day at a time, one task at a time, one conversation at a time.

## A PRACTICAL SUGGESTION

Figuring out where and how to store all this information can be overwhelming. Nancy and I have found Evernote (www.Evernote.com) to be extremely helpful. Evernote is available online and as an app (yes, I know, another app). We have found it to be a fantastic online storage tool. You can create electronic folders and notebooks that allow you to store any and all of your important data. One of the most helpful for us is a record of all repairs and improvements made on our home. I (Dan) have it filed by the project and provided Nancy with the contractor contact information she will need.

You can highlight selected information to be encrypted and password protected. There are different plans available. Their *free* version is certainly enough to get started, while the *personal* and *professional* versions are reasonably priced and offer additional features.

The key is to find something that works for you and then stick with it.

## SOME FINAL THOUGHTS

A few final thoughts about having caring conversations amidst life's biggest disruptions:

**It is a process.** Trying to gather all this information in a short period of time will most likely add additional stress to your relationships. It might be wise to map out a plan for when and how you will collect what you need. Be sure to be sensitive to the work patterns and emotional needs of everyone involved.

**Celebrate small victories.** As you complete pieces of the process, celebrate your accomplishments. Each piece is a step forward. First, consider what is important and valuable to you, where you want to invest your time. Then, when you complete each step, reward yourself with one of the things most valuable to you.

**Ask for help.** Chances are pretty good that people in your orbit can help with each area. Who is a handyman who might help with home care questions? Spending time with a lawyer or financial planner would be invaluable. Is there someone who always seems to be prepared and well-organized? Could they help? Asking people to help with specific pieces of the process will probably be most helpful. If you don't know whom to ask, there is a contributors list on the following pages. These people might not be a bad place to start.

**This is an evolving project.** Planning such as this is never really completed. Once you start, finding other areas you might want to include is common. Chances are really good that you asked, "Why didn't they include this?" as you read the book. Reviewing the information you have collected once a year would be wise. Things will need to be updated, and your thoughts will evolve over time. Maybe set a "trigger" to remind yourself to do it (ex., the week following my birthday).

**When it gets hard, focus on why you are working on this.** A project such as this will get difficult. You will question why you are spending time and effort putting everything together. When this happens, remember it is an investment in supporting those you love. The ultimate goal is to help those we care most about navigate life's biggest disruptions. We want to see them heal and experience the best life has to offer. A little investment of our time can help that process.

**Never stop asking, where is the Spirit in this?** One of the most challenging questions for us will be, "Where is the Spirit of God in the midst of this disruption?" We will often feel alone and abandoned. As you begin each day, invite the Spirit to help you see moments of joy, hope, and promise. Ask for the eyes, ears, heart, and mind to see the struggle of others. Tell the Spirit that while you may not feel blessed, you are willing to be a blessing and look for opportunities to help others.

As you begin to move this way, I am confident that you will see the world with different eyes. You will see the Spirit coming alongside you amid your disruption to lift you up.

May your spirit be open to hearing the "still, small voice" of the Spirit speaking gently yet boldly into your life.

# CONTRIBUTORS

The following people shared their wisdom to help make this project what it is. For all that is good within these pages, we give them credit for being willing to share their insight and experience. I (Dan) take responsibility for any shortcomings. We share the list of contributors in alphabetical order. The contact information connected with their names was accurate at the time of publication.

**John L. Blair:** Partner, DT Investment Partners, LLC – www.dtinvestmentpartners.com - jblair@dtinvestmentpartners.com - 484-778-4425

**Matthew Grieco:** Funeral Director / Funeral Home Owner, Grieco Funeral Home & Crematory – www.griecofunerals.com – mgrieco@griecofunerals.com – 484-734-8100

**Joan Holliday:** Retired Public Health Nurse and Community Organizer with Bridging the Community - www.bridgingthecommunity.org - dochollisv@aol.com

**Rev. Annalie Korengel:** Pastor/Hospice Chaplain, Unionville Presbyterian Church - http://www.unionvillepresbyteri anchurch.org/ - Pastorannalie@gmail.com – 610-952-2992

**Chris Lawrence:** Founder & Executive Director, Hope Has Arrived – www.hopehasarrived.com- chris@hopehasarrived.com

**Paul Maynor:** CFP: 484-905-1212

**Patricia (Tricia) McDermott:** Co-Director / Spiritual Director, Imagine Ministries - www.imagineministries.net - tricia@imagineministries.net

**Daniel Nicewonger**: Spiritual Formation Catalyst, A Place in the Conversation – www.aplaceintheconversation.org - dan@aplaceintheconversation.org – 704-918-8043

**Nancy Nicewonger**: Lead Facilitator, A Place in the Conversation – www.aplaceintheconversation.org - Nancy@aplaceinthecon-versation.org – 704-918-8042

**Rayann Nicewonger**: rjnice99@gmail.com

**Michael R. Perna**, Esquire: Perna & Abracht Law Offices, LLC – www.pa4law.com – mperna@pa4law.com – 610-444-0933

**Christina Reid:** Associate Broker, RE/MAX Town & Country – www.christinareid.com – chrisreid@comcast.net – 610-999-1081

**Rev. Tony Tillford:** Chaplain, Total Health Encouragement Ministries – ttilford55@yahoo.com – 610-812-8911

# PERMISSIONS

**Page 37:** *How Do I Feel* - Excerpt(s) from The Journey Continues: Finding Joy Amidst Life's Struggles by Daniel Nicewonger, copyright © 2022. Used by Permission of Nancy Nicewonger.

**Page 69:** *Can Fear Be My Friend* - Excerpt(s) from The Journey Continues: Finding Joy Amidst Life's Struggles by Daniel Nicewonger, copyright © 2022. Used by Permission of Nancy Nicewonger.

**Page 101:** *Silent Tears* - Excerpt(s) from The Journey Continues: Finding Joy Amidst Life's Struggles by Daniel Nicewonger, copyright © 2022. Used by Permission of Nancy Nicewonger.

**Page 123:** *What is Strength* - Excerpt(s) from The Journey Continues: Finding Joy Amidst Life's Struggles by Daniel Nicewonger, copyright © 2022. Used by Permission of Nancy Nicewonger.

**Page 155:** *Caring Through Isolation* - Excerpt(s) from The Journey Continues: Finding Joy Amidst Life's Struggles by Daniel Nicewonger, copyright © 2022. Used by Permission of Nancy Nicewonger.

**Page 181:** *Loving Through Long-Term Illness* - Excerpt(s) from The Journey Continues: Finding Joy Amidst Life's Struggles by Daniel Nicewonger, copyright © 2022. Used by Permission of Nancy Nicewonger.

# NOTES

## INTRODUCTION

1. Barbara Miller, interview by author, Kennett Square, May 30, 2022.

## CARING FOR THE DYING

1. Henri Nouwen, *You Are The Beloved* (London: Hodder & Stoughton Ltd., 2018), 353.

## 5. LIFE PARTNERS

1. Daniel Nicewonger, "Peace and Chaos," danielnicewonger.com, December 2, 2016, https://danielnicewonger.com/2016/12/02/peace-chaos/.

## HOW DO I FEEL?

1. Daniel Nicewonger, Nancy Nicewonger. "How Do I Feel," *The Journey Continues Finding Joy Amidst Life's Struggles* 2nd ed. (Landenberg: Nicewonger, 2022), 22-23.

## CAN FEAR BE MY FRIEND?

1. Daniel Nicewonger, Nancy Nicewonger. "Can Fear Be My Friend," *The Journey Continues Finding Joy Amidst Life's Struggles* 2nd ed. (Landenberg: Nicewonger, 2022), 95-97.

## 10. NAVIGATING THE HEALTHCARE SYSTEM

1. "Time Allocation in Primary Care Office Visits" National Library of Medicine, accessed March 20, 2023, https://www.ncbi.nlm.nih.gov/pmc/articles/PMC2254573/
2. "15-minute doctor visits take a toll on patient-physician relationships" PBS.org, accessed March 20, 2023, https://www.pbs.org/newshour/health/need-15-

minutes-doctors-time

## 11. Technology / Social Media

1. "Legacy Contacts," Facebook.com/help, accessed July 22, 2022, https://www.facebook.com/help/991335594313139/?helpref=hc_fnav.
2. "Terms of Service," Evernote.com/legal/terms-of-service, accessed February 19, 2023. https://evernote.com/legal/terms-of-service

## Silent Tears

1. Daniel Nicewonger, Nancy Nicewonger. "Silent Tears," *The Journey Continues Finding Joy Amidst Life's Struggles* 2nd ed. (Landenberg: Nicewonger, 2022), 137-138

## What is Strength?

1. Daniel Nicewonger, Nancy Nicewonger. "What Is Strength," *The Journey Continues Finding Joy Amidst Life's Struggles* 2nd ed. (Landenberg: Nicewonger, 2022), 230-231.

## 20. Hospice

1. "What is Hospice?," Hospice Foundation of America.org, accessed December 5, 2022, https://hospicefoundation.org/Hospice-Care/Hospice-Services.
2. "What is Hospice?," Hospice Foundation of America.org, accessed December 5, 2022, https://hospicefoundation.org/Hospice-Care/Hospice-Services.

## Caring Through Isolation

1. Daniel Nicewonger, Nancy Nicewonger. "Caring Through Isolation," *The Journey Continues Finding Joy Amidst Life's Struggles* 2nd ed. (Landenberg: Nicewonger, 2022), 223-224.

## Loving Through Long-Term Illness

1. Daniel Nicewonger, Nancy Nicewonger. "Loving Through Long-Term Illness," *The Journey Continues Finding Joy Amidst Life's Struggles* 2nd ed. (Landenberg: Nicewonger, 2022), 124-126.

## 24. A JOURNEY LIKE NO OTHER

1. Patricia (Tricia) McDermott, "Kit's Health Update," Imagine Ministries December 2022 Newsletter, accessed December 23, 2022, https://www.imagine-ministries.net/newsletter.

Made in the USA
Columbia, SC
12 December 2024

49057662R00126